Pre-Grouping in the
West Midlands

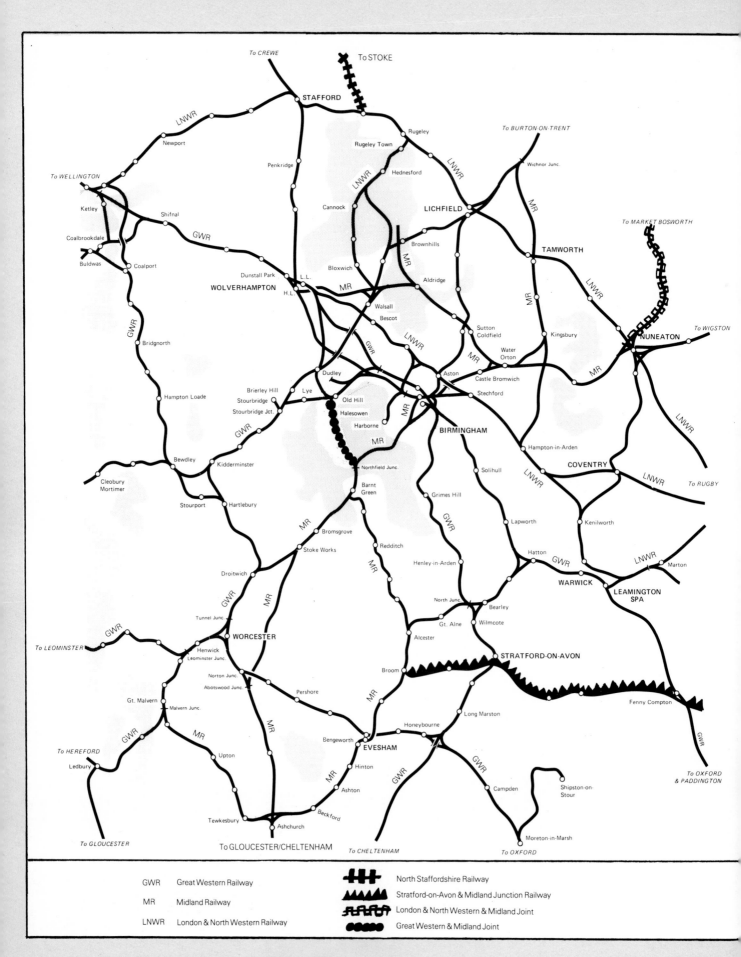

A map of the Grest Western Railway in the West Midlands.

Pre-Grouping
in the
West Midlands

P. B. WHITEHOUSE

OXFORD PUBLISHING COMPANY

ISBN 0-86093-328-8

British Library Cataloguing in Publication Data

Whitehouse, Patrick B.
  Pre-grouping in the West Midlands.
  1. Railroads—England—Midlands—
  History—Pictorial works
  I. Title
  385'.09424   HE3019.M5

Filmset by:
Latimer Trend & Company Ltd, Plymouth, Devon

Printed in Great Britain by:
Balding & Mansell Ltd., Wisbech, Cambs.

Published by:
Oxford Publishing Co.
Link House
West Street
POOLE, Dorset

Bibliography

Railway Reminiscences	G. P. Neele	McCorquodale	1904
Premier Line	O. S. Nock	Ian Allan	1952
The Midland Railway	C. Hamilton Ellis	Ian Allan	1953
History of the Great Western Railway	E. T. MacDermot	Great Western Railway	1927
LMS Engine Sheds (Volume One: LNWR)	Chris Hawkins and George Reeve	Wild Swan	1981
LMS Engine Sheds (Volume Two: Midland Railway)	Chris Hawkins and George Reeve	Wild Swan	1981
Roads and Rails of Birmingham 1900–1939	R. T. Coxon	Ian Allan	
Locomotive and Train Working in the latter part of the Nineteenth Century (Volume Four)	E. L. Ahrons	Heffer	1953
Railways of the West Midlands 1808–1954	C. R. Clinker	Stephenson Locomotive Society	1954
Locomotives of the Great Western Railway		Railway Correspondence and Travel Society	1951–1984
Register of Locomotives of the LNWR	C. Williams		1921
The Locomotives of the LNWR	H. F. F. Livesey	Railway Publishing Co.	1948
Protestant Island	Sir Arthur Bryant	Collins	1967
LNWR, Midland, Great Western Railways	Official Timetables		
The Railway Magazine			
The Engineer			
Great Western Railway Magazine			

Contents

	Plates
Preface and Acknowledgments	—
Some landmarks of West Midland Railway History	—
Introduction	1–41
Birmingham (New Street) Station	42–72
Lines South-West from New Street	73–98
The Lickey Incline	99–111
The Harborne Railway	112–114
Lines to the Black Country	115–128
Birmingham (Snow Hill) Station	129–142
The Great Western South-East of Birmingham	143–174
The LNWR in Coventry and Leamington	175–188
Later Days on the LNWR main line	189–195
Crewe over the Years	196–208
The Rivals—Early Trams and Buses	209–214

Preface and Acknowledgments

This book is the last of a trilogy looking at the railways of the West Midlands in pictorial form, from their beginnings in the 1830s up until Nationalisation. Previous volumes covered the Grouping years of the LMS and GWR, whilst the present book covers the growth period running from Victorian England to the aftermath of what was known as the 'Great War'. The days of LMS, and the post-grouping years of the GWR are times through which I lived myself, and where local knowledge and experiences have been personal; however, in this volume, where everything is in the past tense, this does not apply. Histories of the railway companies per se and of the region as a whole have already been carefully and eruditely written—this book does not purport to be one of them; it is a reflection on the elder days garnished by a collection of photographs and pictures which I have been fortunate enough to gather into my own collection, plus a peep into the archives of local libraries and record offices. To look for facts and tales of life as it was then, I have made use of numerous books in my library, and these are listed in the bibliography. I must, however, make special mention of that magnificent volume of reminiscences written by G. P. Neale, the first superintendent of the Line for the LNWR. Beginning his railway life in the east, he soon came to Walsall and most of his early days were spent in the Birmingham district, making his knowledge of local history and of the men who made it vast, and his stories very human.

I make no claim that readers will find anything new in these pages, but trust that they will reflect the flavour of a period now long gone. To do this, I have received the help of a number of experts in their subjects, and to all of them I would like to express my appreciation. John Edgington of the National Railway Museum has most kindly looked through my text and captions to check historical information, and we both hope that nothing has slipped past. The basis of such information naturally comes from the research of others, and I would particularly like to mention the Stephenson Locomotive Society's *Chronology of Railways in the West Midlands 1808–1954* compiled by that doyen of railway historians, C. R. Clinker. The table of facts of particular West Midlands railway interest has evolved from information obtained from this booklet.

There are many friends whose brains I have picked, and whose photographs I have borrowed including Maurice Bray, Arthur Camwell, Ray Coxon, Lars Davis, A. W. Flowers, C. C. Green, P. Gloster, D. A. C. Harrison and M. Musson. Also, John Burman has kindly allowed me to make use of his father's precious collection of Great Western photographs. Local authorities have also been good enough to look out their records at my request, and acknowledgment to them is included at the foot of the captions concerned. Lastly, I would like to thank the unknown photographers of so many of the illustrations, because if they had not sought to record the passing scenes of nearly a century ago, we would have been much the poorer. Sadly, some of the older photographs are not always to the standard that one would like, but their rarity and interest make inclusion imperative.

P. B. Whitehouse
Birmingham
1984

Some landmarks of West Midland railway history

1837 *4th July* — Grand Junction Railway opens to passengers, from a temporary station at Vauxhall to Stafford, and through to Warrington.

1838 *January* — Grand Junction Railway goods traffic begins—including the world's first Post Office sorting vehicle (horse-box temporarily adapted)—running between Birmingham and Liverpool.

9th April — London & Birmingham Railway opens from Rugby to Birmingham Curzon Street (not officially described as such until 1852).

17th September — London & Birmingham Railway introduces passenger and parcels services from Euston to Birmingham.

12th November — London & Birmingham Railway opens for goods.

1st October — Grand Junction Railway train is revised, to ensure connections with the London & Birmingham Railway.

1839 *January* — Grand Junction Railway is extended into Curzon Street Station.

12th August — Birmingham & Derby Junction Railway opens to public traffic from Derby to Hampton, where it makes a junction with the London & Birmingham Railway thereby instituting a service from Derby to Euston.

1840 *24th June* — Birmingham & Gloucester Railway opens to passengers from Cheltenham to Bromsgrove, whence travellers are taken to Birmingham by horse drawn coach. This route extended to Cofton Farm on 17th September.

1st July — Midland Counties Railway opens from Leicester to Rugby.

17th December — Birmingham & Gloucester Railway extends from Cofton Farm to Camp Hill.

1841 *17th August* — Birmingham & Gloucester Railway opens Camp Hill to Gloucester Junction section, with passenger trains running into Curzon Street. Freight trains terminate (as do some third class passengers conveyed in them) at Camp Hill, which opened on 17th December 1840.

1842 *10th February* — Birmingham & Derby Junction Railway opens from Whitacre to Birmingham (Lawley Street), giving a direct line to Derby. The Hampton line still retains a reduced passenger and freight service. It is converted to single line between August 1842 and May 1843.

14th November — A service of through (first class only) coaches conveys passengers from Euston to Gloucester via Curzon Street.

1844 *10th May* — Midland Railway is formed by amalgamation of North Midland, Midland Counties and Birmingham & Derby Junction Railways.

9th December — London & Birmingham Railway opens the Coventry to Warwick route via Kenilworth.

1846 *1st January* — Formation of the London & North Western Railway as the London & Birmingham, Grand Junction and Manchester & Birmingham Railways begin to act as one system. Confirmed by Parliament in an Act of 16th July q.v.

14th April — Trent Valley Railway is purchased by the above consortium.

17th November — Rugby & Leamington Railway is purchased by the London & North Western Railway.

1847 *12th June* — Connecting spur opens from the London & North Western Railway's Tamworth (Trent Valley) Station to the Midland Railway.

2nd July — Parliament authorises the lease or sale of the Stour Valley Railway from Wolverhampton to Birmingham. Lease to be perpetual to the London & North Western Railway from opening.

1st November — South Staffordshire Railway, worked by the London & North Western Railway, opens from Bescot to Walsall.

1st December — London & North Western Railway Trent Valley line is fully opened from Rugby to Stafford.

1849 *9th April* — South Staffordshire Railway opens from Walsall to Wichnor Junction.

1st May — North Staffordshire Railway opens from Colwich to Stone.

12th November — Shrewsbury & Birmingham Railway opens from Oakengates to Wolverhampton, with the hope of running through to Birmingham over the Stour Valley. This is scuppered by the London & North Western Railway in due course (*see entries below*).

1850 *1st May* — South Staffordshire Railway opens to passengers from Pleck Junction to Dudley, along with the Bescot Curve.

2nd September — London & North Western Railway opens from Coventry to Nuneaton.

1851 *1st March* — London & North Western Railway opens from Rugby to Leamington.

1st May — Midland Railway closes Lawley Street to passengers. Trains use Curzon Street until 1st July 1854.

1852 *February* — Birmingham, Wolverhampton & Stour Valley Railway opens for goods.

1st May — Oxford, Worcester & Wolverhampton Railway opens from Droitwich to Stourbridge.

1st July — Birmingham, Wolverhampton & Stour Valley Railway opens from Wolverhampton to Birmingham, with a temporary platform at the end of what is to be New Street Station.

1st October — Great Western Railway opens to passengers as a mixed gauge line from Banbury to Birmingham.

16th November — Oxford, Worcester & Wolverhampton Railway opens the Stourbridge to Dudley line to passengers.

1853 *February* — Great Western Railway opens from Banbury to Birmingham for goods.

1st May — London & North Western Railway begins a frequent (half-hourly) service over the Stour Valley line as lessees, to ensure the Shrewsbury & Birmingham Railway is excluded.

1st December — Oxford, Worcester & Wolverhampton Railway opens from Dudley to Tipton with a junction, via Tipton Curve, to the Stour Valley line.

1854 *2nd January* — South Staffordshire Railway opens from Sedgley Junction to Dudley Port (Stour Valley).

4th February — Shrewsbury & Birmingham Railway runs three trains each way over the Stour Valley line from Wolverhampton to Birmingham under the Act of 1847, supported by a Court of Chancery judgment, in spite of the effects of London & North Western Railway to exclude the company.

April — Oxford, Worcester & Wolverhampton Railway begins goods workings on the Tipton to Priestfield (standard gauge) and Priestfield to Cannock Road Junction (mixed gauge) routes.

	1st June	London & North Western Railway extension from Curzon Street to New Street is opened, and all regular trains are transferred. The Midland Railway continues to use Curzon Street until 1st July.
	July	Oxford, Worcester & Wolverhampton Railway opens Cannock Road Junction to Bushbury (London & North Western Railway).
	1st July	Oxford, Worcester & Wolverhampton Railway introduces passenger services between Tipton and Priestfield.
		London & North Western Railway/Midland. Curzon Street Station is closed to regular passenger traffic, and Midland Railway trains are transferred to New Street.
	1st September	Shrewsbury & Birmingham and Great Western railways are amalgamated, and the former's running powers on the Stour Valley cease, although trains run until 13th November.
	14th November	Great Western Railway opens from Birmingham to Wolverhampton via Priestfield Junction, in conjunction with the Oxford, Worcester & Wolverhampton Railway
	14th November	Great Western Railway opens from Cannock Road Junction to Stafford Road (Wolverhampton) using mixed gauge.
1855	*October*	Oxford, Worcester & Wolverhampton Railway opens from Priestfield to Wolverhampton (Walsall Street) for goods traffic.
1856	*April*	Oxford, Worcester & Wolverhampton Railway's station at Wolverhampton is renamed Wolverhampton (Low Level).
1858	*February*	Great Western Railway's Birmingham Station is renamed Birmingham (Snow Hill).
	1st February	South Staffordshire Railway opens from Walsall Ryecroft Junction to Cannock.
	14th November	Oxford, Worcester & Wolverhampton Railway opens from Kingswinford Junction to Bromley Basin.
1859	*1st May*	Great Western Railway running time from Birmingham to London is now only 2 hrs. 50 mins., while the London & North Western Railway takes 3 hours.
	11th July	Oxford, Worcester & Wolverhampton Railway opens from Honeybourne to Stratford-on-Avon.
	19th September	Redditch (later the Midland) Railway opens from Barnt Green Junction to Redditch for passengers (opens to goods on 1st October).
	7th November	Cannock Mineral Railway (leased by the London & North Western Railway from the beginning) is opened from Cannock to Rugeley.
1860	*14th June*	Worcester & Hereford and Newport, Abergavenny & Hereford Railways are vested in the Oxford, Worcester & Wolverhampton Railway, becoming the West Midland Railway.
	1st July	Great Western. This is the effective date of an agreement for the GWR's leasing of the Oxford, Worcester & Wolverhampton section of the West Midland Railway.
	10th October	Stratford-on-Avon Railway opens from Hatton Junction to Stratford-on-Avon (mixed gauge). This is vested in the Great Western Railway on 1st July 1883.
1861	*24th July*	The Stratford-on-Avon Railway link with the West Midland Railway is effected.
	1st August	Stratford-on-Avon Railway regular standard gauge passenger service is introduced to Leamington, Honeybourne, Worcester and Malvern.
	1st November	Great Western Railway's connection with the Midland Railway's Camp Hill line opened at Bordesley.

	1st December	London & North Western Railway runs its first train to Burton via Lichfield and Wichnor Junction.
1862	*1st January*	Midland Railway opens from Nuneaton to Hinkley.
		South Leicestershire Railway opens between Nuneaton (London & North Western Railway) and Hinkley. This is extended to Leicester on 1st January 1864.
	2nd June	London & North Western Railway opens from Aston to Sutton Coldfield.
1863	*1st January*	Stratford-on-Avon Railway—all trains are standard gauge as from this date.
	1st April	Stourbridge Railway opens from Stourbridge to Cradley.
	21st July	Redditch Railway ownership is transferred to the Midland Railway.
	14th September	South Staffordshire Railway opens from Tipton Junction to Wednesbury.
1864	*26th January*	London & North Western Railway and Great Western Railway. A connection between the two railways at Leamington is opened.
	1st November	Midland Railway begins passenger services from Whitacre to Nuneaton (opens for goods on 1st December).
1866	*1st January*	Stourbridge Railway opens from Cradley to Old Hill and the Company is transferred to the Great Western Railway on 30th July.
	1st September	Great Western Railway opens Swan Village Junction to Horsley Fields Junction, including the Swan Village Basin.
1867	*1st April*	Great Western route from Old Hill to Galton Junction on the Stour Valley line opens. Also opened is the Smethwick Junction to Handsworth Junction line. Through service from Birmingham (New Street) to Kidderminster and beyond is introduced.
	15th July	South Staffordshire Railway is vested in the London & North Western Railway Stour Valley Railway is vested in the London & North Western Railway. South Leicestershire Railway is vested in the London & North Western Railway.
1868	*4th May*	Evesham & Redditch Railway is opened between Redditch and Alcester.
	1st November	All trains between Birmingham and Wolverhampton are now standard gauge.
1869	*1st April*	Great Western Railway. All sections from Oxford to Wolverhampton are now entirely converted to standard gauge, including the Stratford line.
1870	*1st February*	Stourbridge Railway is vested in the Great Western Railway.
1872	*1st January*	London & North Western Railway goods trains begin to work over the Midland Railway from Wichnor Junction to Derby. Passenger trains follow suit on 1st March.
	1st April	Midland Railway commences the conveyance of third class passengers on all trains.
	1st November	Wolverhampton & Walsall Railway opens and is worked individually by both the London & North Western Railway and Midland Railway. After 1st December it is worked by the Midland Railway alone.
1873	*1st July*	East & West Junction Railway (later the Stratford-on-Avon & Midland Junction Railway) opens from Kineton to Stratford-on-Avon.
1874	*30th July*	Wolverhampton, Walsall & Midland Junction Railway is vested in the Midland Railway.
	10th August	Harborne Railway (worked from outset by the London & North Western Railway) opens from Harborne Junction, on the Stour Valley

		line, to Harborne.
1875	1st January	Midland Railway abolishes second class, and upgrades its third class. In addition, all first class fares are cut to second class levels.
	1st July	Birmingham West Suburban Railway, from King's Norton Junction to Granville Street, is vested in the Midland Railway.
		Wolverhampton & Walsall Railway is vested in the London & North Western Railway.
1876	3rd April	Midland Railway. Birmingham West Suburban line opens.
	1st July	London & North Western Railway and Midland Railway. The Wolverhampton & Walsall line is purchased by the Midland Railway. Trains start running on 1st August.
	4th September	Alcester Railway, worked by the Great Western Railway, opens from Bearley. Agreement is made on 4th September 1877, and vested on 22nd July 1878.
1878	28th February	Midland Railway Kingsbury Branch opens.
	1st March	Great Western Railway opens Dudley to Old Hill and Old Hill to Halesowen.
1879	2nd June	Evesham, Redditch & Stratford Railway opens from Broom to Stratford-on-Avon (East & West Junction Railway) Station. Passenger services were withdrawn on 1st August 1877 between Kineton and Stratford.
	1st July	Midland Railway opens between Castle Bromwich and Walsall.
	1st October	Great Western Railway opens Stourbridge Junction, which is renamed on the same date to Stourbridge Town.
1880	19th July	Midland Railway opens from Nuneaton (Abbey Junction) to Nuneaton (London & North Western Railway).
	7th September	London & North Western Railway opens between Stechford and Aston for goods. Passengers services follow on 1st March 1882.
1881	1st March	London & North Western Railway opens Pleck Junction to Darlaston Junction (then James Bridge Junction).
		London & North Western Railway opens Portobello Junction to Heath Town Junction.
	1st August	Great Northern Railway takes possession of the Stafford & Uttoxeter Railway.
1882		North Staffordshire Railway begins through working of engines and trains to Walsall and Birmingham (New Street).
	1st April	Midland Railway opens Aldridge to Brownhills for goods.
	1st July	Evesham & Redditch Railway is vested in the Midland Railway.
	1st November	Midland Railway opens Brownhills to Cannock Chase for goods.
1883	10th September	Halesowen Railway opens from Halesowen Junction (Midland) to Halesowen.
1884	2nd March	London & North Western Railway opens Kenilworth Junction to Berkswell for goods. Passenger services follow on 2nd June.
	1st July	Midland Railway opens between Aldridge and Brownhills.
	1st September	London & North Western Railway Sutton Coldfield to Lichfield route is opened for goods. A passenger service commences on 15th December.
	7th November	Oldbury Railway opens Langley Green to Oldbury for goods.
1885	8th February	London & North Western Railway and Midland Railway. New Street Station is enlarged with a new side for Midland Railway trains.
	22nd March	East & West Junction Railway, passenger services are restored.
	1st May	Oldbury Railway opens to passengers.
	1st July	Midland Railway opens from Church Road Junction (Birmingham West Suburban Line) to New Street, thus giving through running from Derby via New Street. Granville Street Station closes, and Five Ways opens.
1886	10th August	Oldbury Railway is worked by the Great Western Railway.
1887	1st July	Midland Railway. Granville Street line is extended to Suffolk Street, and Central Goods Station is opened.
1889	1st April	London & North Western Railway opens Soho Loop.
	1st October	London & North Western Railway/Midland Railway. An agreement that all Midland trains will now use the new section of New Street Station.
1890	1st November	London & North Western Railway. Tipton and Wednesbury section closes to passengers.
1892	1st July	Midland Railway. Lifford Curve is opened allowing passenger trains to circulate from New Street and back via Camp Hill and the Birmingham West Suburban lines.
1893	7th May	London & North Western Railway. Old Grand Junction line is raised between Vauxhall and Proof House Junction to allow trains to cross over the track to Curzon Street at high level. Until this date, the latter station was still in use both for London & North Western Railway and Midland Railway excursion trains to and from Sutton Coldfield and Sutton Park respectively.
1894	6th June	Birmingham & Henley-in-Arden Railway opens from Kingswood (later Lapworth) Rowington Signal Box Junction to Henley-in-Arden for passengers. Goods services follow on 2nd July.
	1st July	Oldbury Railway is vested in the Great Western Railway.
1895	1st July	London & North Western Railway reopens the Tipton and Wednesbury section to passengers.
1897	1st July	Great Western Railway loop from Hatton North Junction to Hatton Branch Junction opens.
1900	1st July	Birmingham & Henley-in-Arden Railway is vested in the Great Western Railway.
1902	2nd April	Great Western Railway. Halesowen Basin branch opens to goods only.
1906	30th June	Halesowen Railway is vested jointly in the Great Western Railway and the Midland Railway.
1907	9th December	Great Western Railway opens for goods from Tyseley to Bearley Junction on the North Warwick line. Passenger services commence on 1st July 1908.
1908	22nd March	Midland Railway. Water Orton to Kingsbury direct line opens for goods. Passenger services follow on 3rd May.
	1st July	Great Western Railway. With the opening of the North Warwick line to Stratford via Henley-in Arden, the old station is closed to passengers, and the branch extended to the North Warwick line.
1909	1st July	Great Western Railway. Birmingham (Moor Street) opens for passengers. Goods services commence on 7th July 1914.
1910	1st July	Great Western Railway. Ashendon Junction to Aynho cut-off reduces the Paddington to Birmingham distance from 129 to $110\frac{3}{4}$ miles. Great Western Railway. The company withdraws all second class accommodation.
1912	1st January	London & North Western Railway withdraws all second class accommodation.
1914	10th August	London & North Western Railway loop line from Coventry (Humber Road) Junction to

1915	1st January	Three Spires Junction opens for goods.
		Great Western Railway. Lapworth to Henley-in-Arden is closed to passengers.
	3rd March	Great Western Railway. Oldbury branch is closed to passengers.
	29th March	Great Western Railway. Stourbridge Town branch is closed to passengers.
1916	1st January	Great Western Railway. Lapworth to Henley-in-Arden old station closes. Goods track is removed one year later.
		London & North Western Railway. Tipton and Wednesbury, closes to passengers.
1917	1st January	Midland Railway. Whitacre to Hampton route is closed to passengers.
		Great Western Railway. Bearley to Alcester section is closed entirely.
1919	April	Midland Railway and Great Western Railway, Halesowen joint branch is closed to regular passengers.
	1st May	Great Western Railway. Stourbridge Junction to Stourbridge Town section reopens.
1922	18th December	Great Western Railway. Bearley to Alcester line reopens to Great Alne. On 1st August 1923, the entire stretch reopens.

Introduction

In May 1893 a remarkable, gentle and kindly man set out on the first major leg of an even more remarkable series of railway journeys—travelling from Wolverhampton to London over the tracks of the LNWR to Stafford and the Great Northern (plus a section of the North Stafford) thence via Uttoxeter, Derby, Nottingham and Grantham to King's Cross. He returned to his home in Kidderminster by way of Euston and the LNWR main line to Birmingham, then via the through coach to Tenbury Wells which ran from Birmingham (New Street) to Galton Junction and the GWR. By 1932, when I was beginning my serious interest in railways, T. R. Perkins had achieved his life's ambition of travelling over every line of railway in the British Isles to possess a regular passenger service, a route mileage exceeding 22,000. It was typical of TRP, as he was later known to his many railway friends, that he would always be prepared, not only to pass on his experiences to others who were of his generation and knowledgeable, but also to those of us who were young and who were not. It was easy to sit for evenings on end and listen enthralled to the detailed stories of these travels, but this was not the finish of it as he was a true teacher, who inspired an interest in things which were too far back for us to have ever known bar maybe, the childhood sight of pre-grouping colours in Birmingham (New Street) Station, and French built GWR compounds in Snow Hill. By the early days of British Railways, TRP was an old gentleman but his interest was still there, being enough to ensure that he travelled on Stephenson Locomotive Society specials to cover that odd curve or short section of line not normally used by passenger trains. What an experience it must have been.

Born in 1872, Perkins had been able to mix with those who had seen the London & Birmingham and the Grand Junction Railways opened. He saw the railways build up to their zenith and begin their decline. To him, North Western, Midland, North Stafford, Stratford-upon-Avon and Midland Junction were all day to day names. He was thirteen by the time the second section of New Street Station was opened, and Midland trains actually ran through by means of the tunnels up to Five Ways and the old Birmingham West Suburban Railway.

Perkins' journey to London (setting off heading in the wrong direction—northwards) from Wolverhampton (High Level) Station is a memory in itself, with a 3.30 a.m. start in a crowded Euston to the north express, with sleeping passengers stretched out on nearly every seat and one of Francis Webb's 'Precedent' class 2-4-0 locomotives at its head. One thinks, perhaps, of *Phantom*, with its eldritch screech of a whistle and red hot cinders showering on to the roofs of the leading coaches. Stafford Station was then typical of LNWR practice featuring low platforms, but apart from that little changed until the demise of steam. The first sign of the new age was the closure to passengers of the Great Northern line to Uttoxeter with, in Perkins' day, its green 2-4-0s with chocolate frames and polished brass safety-valves. The branch train would

then have consisted of GNR four or six wheelers with flat roofs, the third class compartments sharing an oil lamp with their neighbours. The rest of the journey out does not come into the compass of this volume covering West Midlands but when writing of his experience in the Railway Magazine, TRP recalls the journey back and of passing the old Midland station at Hampton-in-Arden and wondering what its history might be. That, in truth, was really the beginning.

Before the railways came to the West Midlands, the area was already extremely well served by canal undertakings of some magnitude. This was not an easy matter as Birmingham, a major town even in the early Victorian era, stands some 450 ft above sea level. In the 1820s and early 1830s everything went by water, although it was the coming of the railways—from the north in the form of the Grand Junction and from the south via the London & Birmingham—which began the revolution. This was compounded by the Birmingham & Derby Junction, which met the latter at Hampton. The first train from Birmingham to London is believed to have been driven by Matthew Kirtley, who was to become the Midland Railway's initial Locomotive Superintendent in 1841 at the age of 28. He was certainly appointed Locomotive Foreman for the Birmingham & Derby Junction Railway at Hampton in 1839. The particular growth of railways in the area from that date on has already been set out in tabular form.

There were three large companies which served the West Midlands after the amalgamations of the 1840s and 1850s. These were the London & North Western Railway, the Midland Railway and the Great Western Railway. These were later joined on the periphery by the North Stafford whose engines ran into Birmingham (New Street), and the Great Northern which met the LNWR at Stafford. If one stretched a point, the Great Central Railway tracks at Banbury and Rugby (much later) could be included. Added to these were some rather charming secondary lines including the Stratford-upon-Avon & Midland Junction; the Cleobury Mortimer & Ditton Priors; and the Harborne railways—the first two being worked by their owning companies and the latter by the LNWR.

By the mid-1850s, things had settled down somewhat. The 'Railway Mania' was over, and the LNWR's Captain Mark Huish's piratical tactics had rebounded by driving the Oxford & Birmingham Railway, latterly the GWR (whose trains ran over the spot where, in 1806, some 40,000 people watched Birmingham's only public hanging) into a station then named Livery Street. This was to form a route of some competition, a situation which was to last until Euston finally got its own back in 1967 under British Railways rule. There are still small landmarks in the form of the old arches known as Duddeston Viaducts which, had the original line been completed and opened, would have connected the Oxford & Birmingham with the London & Birmingham at Curzon Street. If this had actually happened, there would have been problems with the eventual extension into New Street, a level crossing on the main lines being inevitable. The great LNWR Superintendent of the line, G. P. Neele, once stated that he heard the Great Western's General Manager remark that the LNWR compelled them to make the viaduct, and when this was completed objected to the junction! The viaduct remains, in part, as a monument to Victorian railway struggles for power in the form of territorial extensions.

Neele, who began his LNWR railway life on the South Staffordshire Railway at Walsall, tells a story of H. P. Bruyeres, the then Superintendent of the London & Birmingham section of the LNWR. Bruyeres was a military martinet known, even in those days, as being unbending and unapproachable:

The Midland Railway, making its connections via Hampton and Rugby, proposed to carry coal and asked the LNWR to take this forward.

"What! Coal by railway" said Mr Bruyeres. "They will be asking us to carry dung next."

"Tell Bruyeres" said George Stephenson "that when we carry him by railway we do carry dung."

The result, it is said, was a temporary compromise and the coal, not more than six wagons at a time and covered by tarpaulins, was taken the shortest distance possible by rail, being transferred to the canal at Crick Station.

Other difficulties had occurred in 1852 with the opening, after much litigation, of the Stour Valley line between Wolverhampton and Birmingham. Having put the fly boats out of operation and given the inhabitants of Tipton, Oldbury and Smethwick (on the banks of the Birmingham Canal) an opportunity of a better local service, the rights of running over the Stour Valley were hotly contested, with both the LNWR and the GWR entering the battle. The outcome of an earlier series of skirmishes had ensured that the Great Western controlled the railway from Shrewsbury to Wellington and Wolverhampton, under the auspices of the Shrewsbury & Birmingham Railway. The latter duly gave notice that they intended to use their authority, granted under former Parliamentary Acts, to run over the Stour Valley line. This was now controlled by the LNWR and in view of this invasion threat, the LNWR contended that such powers did not apply to the GWR. The Shrewsbury company then tried to force the issue by utilising its running powers. However, on arrival at Wolverhampton, its passage was blocked by a LNWR engine, appropriately named *Hotspur*. The two engines met buffer to buffer, and neither pushing nor pulling had any effect. Matters got even worse and contractors' navvies were called in to take up the rails, and other engines were derailed to make sure of the job. Eventually, a large body of the constabulary arrived, and the Mayor prepared to read the Riot Act.

In the event the case was referred to arbitration and no doubt, the lawyers had a fine time of it. By 1854, the GWR had completed their own line into Snow Hill and joined up with the Birmingham & Oxford Railway, so the LNWR won in the end. But this did not stop the war between Shrewsbury and Wolverhampton. The other company taken into the LNWR network was the South Staffordshire Railway, running from Walsall to Dudley and Walsall to Lichfield. This also covered mining interests, joining the Grand Junction at Bescot. Its trains also ran into Curzon Street, hence the naming of a section of No. 1 platform at New Street, the South Stafford bay.

The General Manager of the South Staffordshire company was John Douglas Payne, who had come from the Birmingham & Gloucester Railway which was formed in 1836. It was he who took the credit for having played a leading part in checking the extension of the broad gauge at Gloucester. The original line from Bristol to Gloucester was built to Brunel's 7 ft. 0 in. gauge whilst the Birmingham section was built to the standard gauge, so naturally both parties had an interest in their own status quo.

When the Parliamentary Committee, set up to decide on the whole question of gauge, visited Gloucester to inspect the alleged confusion which occurred during the change of gauge, Payne got wind of it and hurried down to be ready for them. Just in case the extent of the transfer work appeared to be too small, Payne arranged for the unloading of two trains already dealt with, in addition to the work in hand. When the MPs came to the scene, they were naturally appalled by the well-contrived clamour arising from the shouting out of addresses of consignments, the throwing of packages from wagon to wagon, and the many enquiries for missing articles. The result was to stop further progress northward of the broad gauge.

Both the Midland Railway and the LNWR penetrated the directorship of the South Staffordshire Railway, and both companies worked from Walsall to Wolverhampton, the Midland getting there via the Sutton Park branch from Water Orton on the old Birmingham & Derby line. There was an accident at Dudley Port on 29th July 1853 where the South Staffs to Dudley passed below the Stour Valley, and where there were separate high and low level stations. A passenger train which had stopped at the low level station was waiting for a connection from Stour Valley when it was run into by a freight train from Great Bridge. Its driver contested that the distant signal was not at danger. There was no satisfactory answer, but it transpired that a porter was standing in for the signalman and the levers were at the far end of the platforms, where passengers could have interfered with them. Similar laxity occurred at Wednesbury within a couple of months, when signalling and signal discipline was still in its infancy. The following year there was another serious collision close to Walsall Station when the railway was heavily criticised by the Board of Trade, on the basis that the signals had been 'given' by a platelayer and a thirteen year old girl. It transpired that the LNWR driver had never been over the line before, and the men involved had been on duty for 19, 21 and 26 hours at a stretch.

By now another company was entering the lists, this being the Oxford, Worcester & Wolverhampton Railway which had reached Stourbridge in 1852, and Dudley by 1853. Nicknamed, rightly at the time, 'the Old Worse and Worse', the line was naturally an unwelcome intruder for the GWR, which was already in Birmingham by means of the Oxford & Birmingham Railway, although this was of mixed gauge. It is of interest today that the 1853 expresses via Didcot took 2 hours 45 minutes, while the LNWR time over a shorter route was 3 hours. At that time the Great Western controlled two empires, one based on Swindon and the other on Wolverhampton, using the 7 ft. 0 in. and 4 ft. 8 in. gauges respectively. The Northern division at Wolverhampton was allowed a larger degree of independence, despite coming under the overall auspices of the Chief Engineer at Swindon. The first standard gauge engines on the GWR were, in fact, those taken over from Shrewsbury & Chester and Shrewsbury & Birmingham companies, when these became part of the system in 1854. The new factory at Wolverhampton began building engines in 1859. The Oxford, Worcester & Wolverhampton workshops at Worcester had opened in 1854, these passing into the ownership of the West Midland Railway (incorporating the Oxford, Worcester & Wolverhampton; Newport, Abergavenny & Hereford; and the Worcester & Hereford companies) in 1860, the whole being taken by the GWR in 1863.

Meanwhile 1854 saw the opening of New Street Station, Birmingham, where among other innovations the electric telegraph was employed for controlling traffic at both ends of the station. From the Grand Junction signal box at the south end to Sheepcote Lane box, near Monument Lane, to the north. This was the *sole* length of the telegraph system in the Birmingham district at that time.

The year 1854 also saw the closure of Curzon Street passenger station, except for occasional excursion trains.

On the Great Western Railway, Birmingham passengers going

north had to wait until the same year before they could join the Oxford, Worcester & Wolverhampton at Priestfield Junction, and thus make their way into Wolverhampton. The stage was set for the GWR's Paddington to Chester main line and its eventual entry into Mid-Wales. The great name of Snow Hill did not exist until 1858, as it was earlier known as Livery Street or Great Charles Street. Other links with the OW&W came via Stratford (standard gauge), where the mixed gauge from Hatton to Shakespeare's birthplace was opened to trains by means of the Stratford Railway in 1860. From 1863, these were standard gauge only. The third rail between Oxford and Wolverhampton should have been taken out completely in 1868, but there were delays due to non-completion of new stock so from 1st November, all passenger trains between Birmingham and Wolverhampton, with the exception of one express each way between Oxford and Birmingham, were all standard gauge. These two passenger and four goods services in each direction, three of which ran from Victoria Basin at Wolverhampton, continued to be broad gauge until the end of March 1869, after which the third rails north of Oxford were removed.

The main West Midlands network having been established, other important links appeared including Aston to Sutton Coldfield and on to Lichfield, the branch to Harborne (a separate company, but worked by the LNWR) and the line from Halesowen Junction to Halesowen then on to Old Hill, where it joined the GWR between Galton Junction and Stourbridge Junction. Where new companies were formed, their lines were worked and generally acquired by either the LNWR, GWR or Midland Railway.

G. P. Neele tells an interesting story of a happening at Leamington during one of his journeys with the Royal Train in 1874. On 20th May of that year Her Majesty had left Windsor for the north as late as 7.55 p.m., and was travelling via the Great Western to Wolverhampton where the Royal Train would be transferred to the LNWR. For some reason special instructions had been issued to keep all the stations en route quite private and consequently, no one was allowed on any platforms. There was to be a stop at Leamington for water, and here a problem arose in the form of Lord Aylesford who turned up in his Volunteer uniform determined to be on the platform despite all orders to the contrary. He would brook no denial, and insisted on his right and title to be admitted. The GWR staff, caps in hand, told his Lordship that their District Superintendent was on the station, and that it was more than their job was worth to admit him. Lord Aylesford then demanded to see that great man, who accordingly went to the locked gates and told the irate nobleman what was what:

'And pray who are you' said his Lordship.
'I am the superintendent of this division of the Great Western Railway.'
'And where do you come from?'
'Birmingham.'
'Oh' with supreme contempt. 'Birmingham—I thought so.'
But whatever his Lordship might or might not have felt about Birmingham or a Birmingham man, he did not get in that night and was left swearing at the gate.

The Midland Railway obtained through running from north to south-west in 1885, when it took the Birmingham West Suburban Railway from Lifford to Granville Street and extended it down through Five Ways and the tunnels into the newly-built south side of the station. Although at that time it had a joint status with the LNWR, the partners were not always friends, and this feeling continued well into LMS days and even beyond. With all the connections provided by both companies, Birmingham (New Street) became a major interchange point, and remains so to this day.

As far as the Great Western Railway was concerned, probably the less said about the old Snow Hill station the better—it had a single through passenger platform in each direction, with bay platforms at the north and for Wolverhampton and Stourbridge local services and through goods lines. There was a wrought iron and glass overall roof, this being a paler imitation of New Street. The same thing could be said about the train services with the initials GWR being aptly, if rudely, construed as 'Great Way Round'. Ahrons, in his epic writings *Locomotive and Train Working in the Nineteenth Century* reckoned that north of Oxford, as far as Birmingham and Wolverhampton in the 1880s, there was still a considerable amount of 'baulk' road although a large part was laid on the usual transverse sleepers. This old track was very stiff, so much so that the engines were 'two coaches better' when travelling over the transverse sleeper sections. In addition, the Civil Engineer's department had economised on rails by turning over the old ones near Fenny Compton and down Harbury Bank; the effect of this being that where the wheels ran over the slight indentations made by the chairs, there were nasty and prolonged chattering noises. Matters improved within the next decade and by 1892, the GWR was running its first corridor train from Paddington to Birmingham, Wolverhampton and Birkenhead with 1st, 2nd and 3rd classes. The first non-stop run between Paddington and Leamington was introduced in 1898 taking 2 hours 27 minutes although by 1899, this had improved further with the 2.10 p.m. 'up' Birmingham express (via Didcot) producing a journey time of 2 hours 25 minutes, while slipping a coach at Leamington. This was to compete (the best it could with its longer route) with the LNWR, whose Euston to Birmingham expresses (the faster ones), took only 2 hours 5 minutes by 1902.

The LNWR had, by now, styled itself 'the Premier Line' and where its track was concerned, this was probably reasonable although some passengers would not have felt this appropriate as far as their comfort was concerned. Its first two hour expresses (four 'down' and three 'up') appeared in 1905 by which time George Whale had been able to introduce his new 'Precursor' class 4-4-0 locomotives, which revitalised the LNWR motive power. The year 1910 saw the 7.50 a.m. from Wolverhampton (8.20 a.m. from Birmingham) service running to London (Broad Street), this including the provision of a stenographer for the convenience of businessmen.

Also in 1910, the GWR came into its own, having opened a cut-off line from Ashendon Junction to Aynho Junction, south of Banbury. This reduced the distance from Paddington to Birmingham (Snow Hill) from 129 miles, via Didcot, to 110 miles. Thus after five hard years, two hour expresses between London and Birmingham were able to be introduced. This was helped by yet another motive power revolution, with the entry on to the scene of the renowned George Jackson Churchward. Thus the great period of railway progress was, at last, under way.

By the end of the first decade of the new century the GWR was well into a massive modernisation and expansion scheme involving the quadrupling of its tracks from Handsworth Junction through Snow Hill to the new station at Tyseley. It was here that they met the virgin North Warwickshire line running to Bearley West Junction, hence completing a direct link to Stratford, Cheltenham, Gloucester and Bristol. At the same time, the opportunity was taken to reconstruct Birmingham (Snow Hill), the result being probably the finest station to grace the West Midlands. It was efficient, airy and topped by the Great Western Hotel. There are many who still mourn its passing under British Railways. With the North Warwick line providing extra traffic, the opportunity was taken to open a new suburban terminus at Moor Street for both passengers and goods. The passenger station remains today.

Little changed outwardly from this period on to Grouping although now that we have hindsight, there were clear indications that the railways' monopoly was coming to an end. In London, the underground and tube services were already in action, and it was obvious that suburbia was to spread and sprawl contingent with current prosperity to outside the capital, this meant more surface transport. In Birmingham and the West Midlands generally, suburban lines carried plenty of traffic even with the coming of the new tramway systems, but the railways catered best for those living a few miles from the city centre using, for example, the LNWR route to Sutton, the GWR's Acocks Green, Olton and Solihull main line to the south-east and the new North Warwick section. Passengers living in the suburbs of Moseley, Edgbaston and Harborne were adequately served, but generally there was a lack of connections from house door to city centre; with similar situations applying in the fast growing Coventry and Wolverhampton areas. Today, it is hard to grasp how quick and efficient local tramway systems were, with stops every few hundred yards and clear roads right to the hearts of the big towns.

World War I saw some comparatively minor retrenchment when, for example, the reasons for the closures of branches and stations were to release staff and equipment for war purposes although indeed, there were some re-openings, for example the Stourbridge Junction to Stourbridge Town line in 1919. Another wartime loss was the 8.20 a.m. Birmingham (New Street) to London (Broad Street) businessman's express, this service never returning after the war. Strangely, the Midland and Great Western railways joint line, and its trains from King's Norton to Halesowen, did not close to regular passengers until 1919, although unadvertised morning and evening services continued, however, for another four decades.

The Railways Act of 19th August 1921 placed the West Midlands companies into two of the 'Big Four', with the Great Western Railway remaining unchanged but with the London North Western, Midland, North Stafford, Stratford-upon-Avon & Midland Junction and Harborne railways being vested in the London Midland Scottish Group. The Halesowen Joint line automatically became the property of both the GWR and LMS. It was to be a quarter of a century of unease and war before these large groups also died, when the nationalised colossus took over from 1st January 1948.

The change which the railways wrought on the British social scene during the period covered by this book was vast. Glances at the earliest copies of the *Illustrated London News* (some of whose pages have been used to provide earlier illustrations for this book) show an England of squires and smocked peasants, unpaved roads and stage coaches. Travel from London to Birmingham by the Tantivy Mail, on such paved roads as there were, took twelve hours for the distance of 120 miles and, if one went on to Liverpool, another eleven, this being the very fastest journey. With the coming of the Grand Junction Railway the Birmingham to Liverpool time was reduced, in 1837, to four and half hours. In the 1840s Britain was still regional in its outlook although by the 1850s it was knit into one nation by threads of steel and from that time on, when the network was established, there was comparatively little growth in track mileage. In the West Midlands, the great engineering workshops of the world prospered and grew in their second industrial revolution and from Victoria to Edward, and on to the beginning of George V's reign, the railways of the region served its people well.

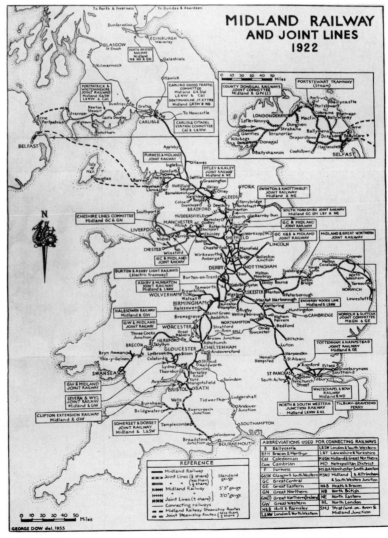

A general map of the Midland Railway at the close of the period, clearly showing the complex of lines directly available to travellers from the Birmingham area.

British Railways

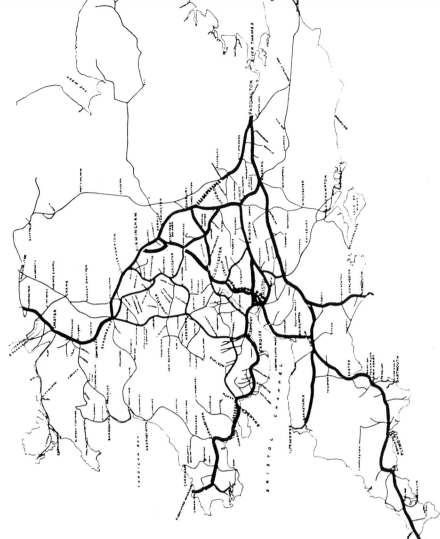

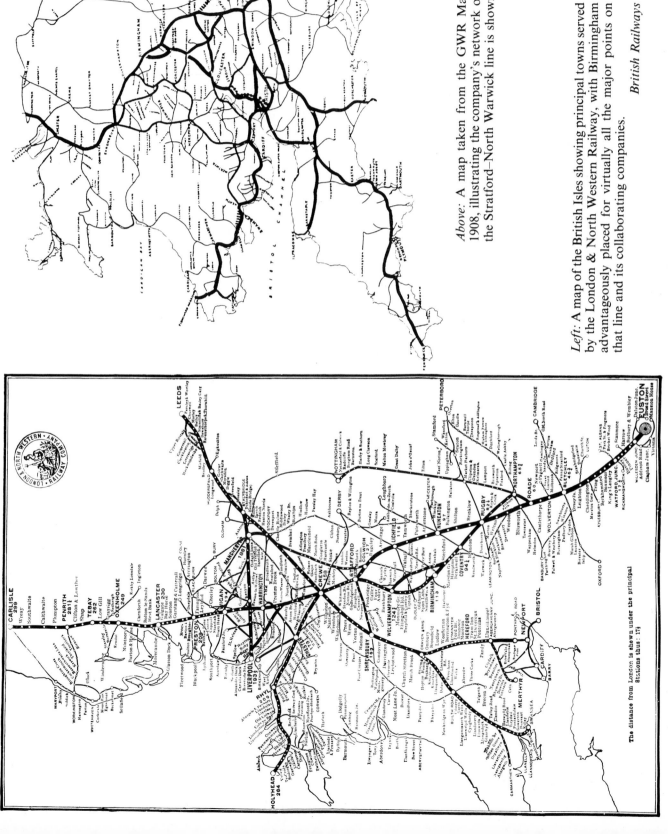

Above: A map taken from the GWR Magazine, November 1908, illustrating the company's network of routes. Note that the Stratford–North Warwick line is shown as completed.

British Railways

Left: A map of the British Isles showing principal towns served by the London & North Western Railway, with Birmingham advantageously placed for virtually all the major points on that line and its collaborating companies.

Plate 2 (below): A reproduction from a London & North Western Railway official coloured postcard showing the London & Birmingham Railway's train shed and office building at Curzon Street Station in 1838.

Ian Wright Collection

BIRMINGHAM STATION · 1838.

late 4 (below): Birmingham, after Liverpool and Manchester, was one of the first big cities to be served by
...il when a temporary station was opened at Vauxhall, on the Grand Junction Railway, on 4th July 1837.
...he next year, 1838, saw the London & Birmingham Railway line open to Curzon Street Station. This print
... a 2-2-0 shows Bury's standard passenger locomotive of 1837–39, used on the London & Birmingham
...ailway as its No. 1.

Millbrook House Collection

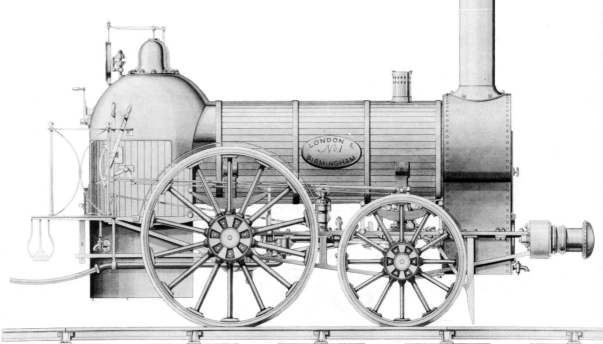

LONDON TO BIRMINGHAM — STATIONS (Table a)

(Facsimile timetable, "LONDON TO BIRMINGHAM" with columns of Mixed, Mail, First Class trains and FARES. Column of Distance from London in Miles.)

Stations listed: LONDON, HARROW, WATFORD, BOXMOOR, B. HAMPSTEAD, TRING, LEIGHTON, BLETCHLEY, WOLVERTON, ROADE, BLISWORTH, WEEDON, CRICK, RUGBY, BRANDON, COVENTRY, HAMPTON, BIRMINGHAM.

There is a Mixed Train from Aylesbury to London at 11 a.m., and one from London to Aylesbury at 3 p.m.

SUNDAY TRAINS.—Times of Departure, Mixed 8 a.m., Mail 9½ a.m., Mixed to Wolverton 6 p.m., Mail, mixed 8¼ p.m.

Children under Ten Years of age, Half-price. Infants in arms, unable to walk, free of charge.—Soldiers *en route* are charged under a special agreement.—Dogs are charged for any distance not exceeding 30 miles, 1s.; 55 miles, 2s.; 85 miles 3s.; and the whole distance, 4s. No dogs allowed to be taken inside the Carriages.

Carriages and Horses should be at the Stations a quarter of an hour before the time of departure, and they cannot be forwarded by any train unless there, at the least, five minutes before its time of departure, which time is punctually observed, and after the doors are closed no Passengers can be admitted.

To guard against accident and delay, it is especially requested that Passengers will not leave their seats at any of the Stations except Wolverton (half way), where ten minutes are allowed for refreshment.

A Passenger may claim the seat corresponding to the number on his Ticket, and when not numbered he may take any seat not previously occupied.—No Gratuity, under any circumstances, is allowed to be taken by any Servant of the Company.

Ten minutes are allowed at the Wolverton Central Station, where a female is in attendance, where refreshments may be obtained.

The Trains marked with an asterisk (*) are in conjunction with those of the Grand Junction Railway; sufficient time being allowed at the Birmingham Station, where refreshments are provided, and waiting rooms, with female attendants.

BRISTOL TO BIRMINGHAM (Table b)

(Facsimile timetable headed "BRISTOL TO BIRMINGHAM", WEEK DAYS / SUNDAYS, with Fares from Bristol 1st 2d 3d classes, and Miles. Advertisements appear at right: BELVOIR HOTEL, Malvern; "TINY CLEE'S" SMOKING MIXTURE; BOARDING HOUSE, Cheltenham; COMMERCIAL & FAMILY HOTEL; FOWLER'S Wine and Spirits; SHIRER AND SONS; CHAMBERLAIN'S ROYAL PORCELAIN WORKS, Worcester; FORD BROTHERS' SLATE WORKS, Gloucester; FRANK AND ELIZABETH HOLYOAKE; CHATEAU MARGAUX, CADIZ WINE COMPANY, London.)

NOTE.—(a) The 7.0 mor. Train from Bristol is 3d Class to Chester, Manchester, and Liverpool, and 1st and 2d Class between Blackwell and Birmingham on Thursdays.

TABLE OF FARES FROM LONDON TO BIRMINGHAM AND LIVERPOOL, AND FROM STATION TO STATION (Table c)

N.B.—The fares by the Night Trains are something more than those enumerated below.

(Triangular facsimile fare chart. Stations down the left column: HARROW, WATFORD, BOXMOOR, BERKHAMPSTD., TRING, LEIGHTON, WOLVERTON, ROADE, BLISWORTH, WEEDON, CRICK, RUGBY, BRANDON, COVENTRY, BIRMINGHAM, WOLVERHMPTN., STAFFORD, WHITMORE, CREWE, HARTFORD, WARRINGTON, LIVERPOOL or MANCHESTER. Across the top, diagonal stepped columns headed London, Harrow, Watford, Boxmoor, Berksted, Tring, Leighton, Wolvrton, Roade, Bliswrth, Weedon, Crick, Rugby, Brandon, Coventry, Birmngm, Wolvrhtn, Stafford, Whtmore, Crewe, Hartford, each with 1st and 2d Class fares in s. d.)

Plates 5–7: These three tables show the times a[nd] fares of trains emanating from the Birmingham ar[ea] around 1840 and in 1858. Taking inflation and t[he] value of the pound over the years into account, [it] shows clearly that travel was not cheap and the vi[tal] role, if the railway was to be of true use to the pub[lic] at large, of the Parliamentary train at 1d per mile.

Dates of Tables;
a. London to Birmingham 1843
b. Bristol to Birmingham 1858
c. Fares list 1840s

P. B. Whitehouse Collecti[on]

Plate 8: This drawing was reproduced in *The Illustrated London News* of 17th November 1849 with the following text:

OPENING OF THE SHREWSBURY AND BIRMINGHAM RAILWAY

On Monday last, this new line of railway was opened with a train of upwards of fifty carriages, accompanied by a fine band of music, and decorated with a profusion of flags and banners.

The train left Shrewsbury at about half-past eight o'clock. It was joined by a considerable number of passengers both at Upton Magna and Walcot, and a large posse of Wellingtonians fell in at that populous town, where the train was received with a volley of cheers, the station and public buildings streaming with flags. Accumulated hundreds joined the train at Oakengates, where a considerable stoppage was required; after which the long body of carriages entered the tunnel, at a slow rate, and was about five minutes in its transitory eclipse. The excavations on both sides of the tunnel, through rock and shale, show the immensity of labour in this part of the line, independent of the construction of the tunnel itself. The rate of the train, from its great weight and length, where there was a slight ascent in the incline, was necessarily slow—with the two powerful and splendid engines, 'Salopian' and 'Wrekin' (and another, we believe, added a portion of the way); but we approached Shiffnal at a better rate; and here, as we

advanced, the view of the town on the flanks of the elevated archway, with the flower-gardens of the house coming up to and abutting on the masonry of the viaduct, presented a singularly beautiful and pleasant scene of active life, excited by the novelty of the occasion. The Shiffnal Station is an extremely neat and tasteful edifice, light and commodious, and was resplendent with flags; and from this town was derived another considerable addition to the passenger-train, in a number of gentlemen and ladies, as well as other humbler and well-dressed classes. The sub-stations of Albrighton and Codsall are pretty edifices; the former being the centre of several other villages, and a considerable population.

At Wolverhampton the crowds of people to receive the train were immense; and it had to thread its way up to the temporary platform amid the cheers of the people, the pealing bells, and rolling drums, &c. of the band—a most glorious and animated scene. It is the first instance of a railway coming up into the large, flourishing, and populous town of Wolverhampton—the rising Birmingham of Staffordshire, and was an object of interest and eclat in proportion.

The train having poured out its living load the engines 'Salopian' and 'Wrekin' were sent to take in water for the return steam, and then speed off with a similar load of the inhabitants of Wolverhampton, including several of the chief corporators of that town, to Shrewsbury, and bring the same back again before the Salopians returned.

Obedience to the "signals" used on a railway is indispensable to the safe passage of a train. A moment's inattention to any one of their significant monitions may be followed by the instant death of heedless unsuspecting multitudes, while, on the other hand, a due observance of them at all times, in all seasons, by night as well as by day, divests the speed of even the fastest pleasure train of danger. It is, of course, most important that the servants of a line should become practically familiar with the things signified by the symbols used in their several establishments, but we also deem it to be of much consequence that the public itself should be acquainted with them, for, were such the case, we should cease to hear of the difficulty of obtaining evidence against negligent servants, which on occasions of accident has ordinarily prevailed. Every traveller would then be an observer and a judge of the means used for his preservation, and in proportion to the vigilance of his survey would be the attention of servants entrusted with duties so important to the lives and limbs of passengers.

The signals used on railways are of great variety. Most of the lines have systems peculiar to themselves; and, in consequence, no uniform observance prevails between them, which is a practice much to be regretted, as it tends to confuse the observation of men engaged on different lines, and of engineers who change one service for another. It cannot, however, be expected that so complicated an operation, and one, too, which has grown up under the management of independent companies, should speedily reach perfection. For the present, the signals are necessarily different on different lines; but we hope to see the day, when the set, which experience has proved the best, shall be universally and compulsorily adopted. We shall now describe the signals used on the more important lines.

Those observed on the London and Birmingham Railway demand the first attention. They consist of Police Signals—Signals shown at Intermediate Stations and the Long Tunnels; and the Engine Signals.

1. POLICE SIGNALS.—When the line is clear, and no obstruction in the way of the onward course of the train is either seen or *suspected*, the policeman stands erect, with his flags in his hand, but showing no signal. See Fig. 1. If it be required that the engine should slacken speed, and proceed with caution, from another engine having passed on the same line within five minutes, a Green Flag is held up in the manner shown in Fig. 2. If it be desired that the engine should slacken speed, and proceed with caution, from any defect in the rails, the Green flag is lowered, and held as shown in Fig. 3. But if it be necessary that the engine should stop altogether at any given point, a Red Flag is shown, and

JUNCTION SIGNAL-MAN AT WORK.

BIRMINGHAM—"ALL CLEAR."   "SLACKEN SPEED—ENGINE."   "CAUTION—RAILS."   DOVER—"CAUTION—RAILS."

2. SIGNALS SHOWN AT INTERMEDIATE STATIONS AND THE LONG TUNNELS.—Signal posts are erected on the "up" and "down" lines at the Intermediate Stations, and at the entrance of Primrose-hill, Watford, and Kilsby Tunnels, showing a Red Board of a large size, and a Green Board of a smaller size, as day signals. A Green or Red Light is substituted as night signals. On a train or engine *passing* an intermediate station, the Green signal is exhibited for the space of *ten* minutes, to denote that a train on the same line has passed within that period, and therefore due

caution must be observed on the part of the drivers and guards. On a train *stopping* at an intermediate station, the Red Signal is shown, and continued for five minutes after its departure, when the Green Signal is turned on, to complete the ten minutes' precautionary signal. On a train entering one of the tunnels, the Red signal is shown for the space of ten minutes, to prevent another engine entering within that time; unless the policeman can previously see through that the line is clear, when the Red Signal will be turned off, and the Green shown, to complete the ten minutes' signal.

Plates 9 & 10: Two reproductions from *The Illustrated London News* (1844) showing the work of early railway policemen/signalmen—hence the nickname 'bobbies'.
Millbrook House

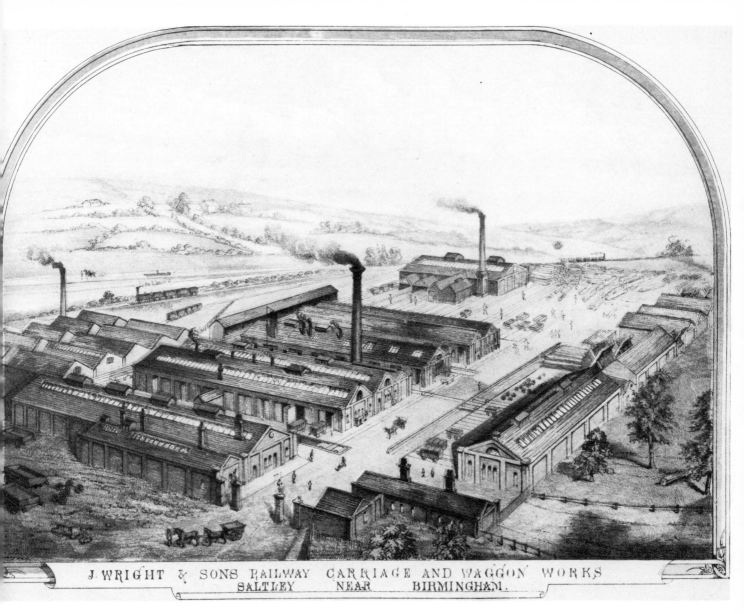

J. WRIGHT & SONS RAILWAY CARRIAGE AND WAGGON WORKS
SALTLEY NEAR BIRMINGHAM.

Plate 11: An early print from Birmingham City Reference Library showing an advertisement for J. Wright & Sons Railway Carriage and Waggon Works, circa 1858, although the drawing itself is of an earlier period. Note that the caption states Saltley *near* Birmingham. The line in the background is very early Midland (Birmingham & Derby Junction). Though much reduced in size and modernised, these works, as Metropolitan-Cammell Limited are still there.

City of Birmingham Public Libraries

Plate 12: A drawing, taken from *The Illustrated London News* of 1846, purporting to show the chaos at Gloucester when transferring livestock from the Midland Railway's standard gauge tracks to the GWR's 7 ft. 0 in. gauge.

Millbrook House Collection

Plate 13: A drawing of the Royal Train on the Midland Railway at Cheltenham in 1849. Queen Victoria was then on her way to Gosport from Balmoral, using the LNWR's state saloon for the first section of the journey. The train had come from Cupar Angus via Newcastle and Darlington, having crossed the Tweed at Berwick by a temporary bridge, halted at Derby for the night and made its way to Birmingham via Whitacre, Hampton and the London & Birmingham line, taking this apparently unusual route to Cheltenham to avoid the Queen being shunted in the 'lift'. Until 1st May 1851, all Midland Railway trains from Derby ran into the terminus at Lawley Street, and any through vehicles from the Derby to Bristol lines had to be conveyed via a transfer track under the LNWR arches at the end of the Lawley Street Viaduct, and down or up in the 'lift'. From Cheltenham, the train proceeded to Gloucester, where Her Majesty was transferred to the GWR and the broad gauge. The second coach from the rear is the early LNWR Royal Saloon, while the end vehicle is possibly Queen Adelaide's.

Millbrook House

Plates 14 & 15: The seals of companie later vested in the GWR. The first two ar from the Birmingham & Oxford Junctio Railway and the Shrewsbury & Birm ingham Railway, both of 1846, while th third is from the Oxford, Worcester & Wolverhampton (Old Worse & Worse from 1852 and the last is of the Wes Midland Railway 1860.

Plate 16: An accident at Elwell's Pool on the LNWR, South Staffs Railway section, in 1859. This spot is to the rear of what is now Bescot Diesel Depot. It is believed that the locomotives are LNWR (Southern Division) Sharp 0-6-0s of 1848.

Walsall Library

Plate 17: A McConnell 0-4-2 tank, No. 734, at Sutton Coldfield sometime in the 1860s. This class was one of three built at Wolverton from 1860 onwards, and anticipated Stroudley's classic use of this wheel arrangement on the LB&SCR Brighton expresses by nearly twenty years. Sutton Coldfield Station was new at the time, and the line from here to Aston opened in June 1862.

Crown Copyright, National Railway Museum

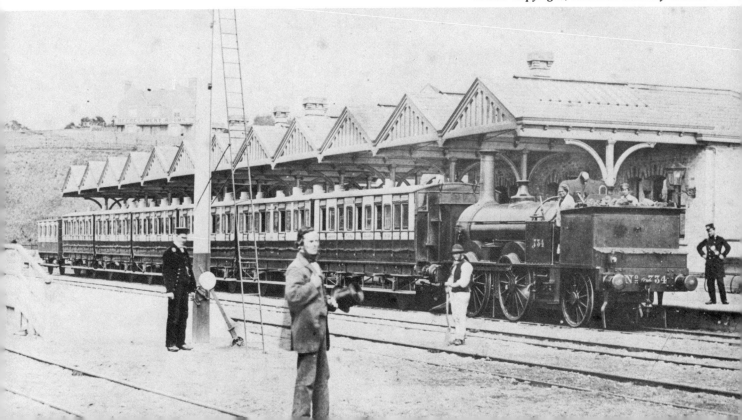

Plate 18: A train crosses the river Severn in 1864 at Dowles Bridge, Bewdley, on the Bewdley to Tenbury Wells line. The locomotive is 2-4-0 tank No. 1A, built at Wolverhampton in 1864 and renumbered 17 in 1865. It was short-lived in this form and was rebuilt as a saddle tank in October 1867, being withdrawn in March 1889.

P. B. Whitehouse Collection

Plate 19: Nailsworth Station in 1873, this being the terminus of the Midland Railway's branch from Stroud. The 0-6-0 tank locomotive is possibly one of the Kirtley 1870s rebuilds of early 1850s tender types.

Crown Copyright, National Railway Museum

Plate 20: This photograph of Hampton-in-Arden Station is not only fascinating but unique. It came into the author's hands via that doyen of railway photography, W. A. Camwell. Hampton-in-Arden was the junction which allowed the Birmingham & Derby Junction Railway (later part of the Midland Railway) to make a connection with the London & Birmingham Railway, thus giving access to London. This began in 1839, and the passenger service was finally withdrawn in 1917. The B&DJ opened from Whitacre to Birmingham (Lawley Street) in 1842, but the Hampton-in-Arden line still retained five 'down' and three 'up' trains. The line was originally double but was singled in that year, and once the Midland Railway was formed and the main line to London opened, the Whitacre to Hampton-in-Arden line was really an anachronism.

The picture is difficult to date, and the unusual fact thrown up is the name Derby Junction clearly seen on the building to the right, which still stands today. The canopy on the left is certainly LNWR of the late Victorian period, but this station was closed and replaced on 28th July 1884. The locomotive on the right is a double-framed 0-6-0 and therefore of the Midland Railway, whilst that on the left is a drop smokebox front LNWR engine; the signal, faintly visible over the top of the Midland engine, is definitely slotted and the branch can be seen curving off to the right. This is a much bigger station than popularly imagined, and one wonders why the apparent LNWR train is in the branch platform.

It is a reasonable assumption that the island platform and track were LNWR. Note the ballast that is nearly up to rail level, indicating the possible mid-1870s period. The locomotive appears to have a headlamp at the chimney base, and the train must therefore be one of the local services terminating at Hampton-in-Arden at that time.   *P. B. Whitehouse Collection*

Plate 21: A composite photograph of GWR Swindon-built No. 311 at Harbury Cutting. The date of the photograph is not certain, but it is likely to be the winter of 1876/7 when local newspapers reported a serious landslip which caused the 'up' line, on the far side of the picture, to be blocked for several months. The appearance of the cutting sides to the right of the tunnel entrance is consistent with this hypothesis. No. 311 was renewed (in engineering terms, a new engine) in April 1884, and the photographer was N. Briggs of Leamington Spa.   *Warwick County Museum*

Plate 22: An early North Staffo[rdshire] Railway locomotive, built by t[he] Worcester Engine Works Co. Ltd. [as] their No. 7 in 1866. It was rebuilt [in] 1890 and scrapped in Decemb[er] 1910. This engine was one of a bat[ch] of ten, with Nos. 90–99 being co[n]structed in 1867. The works we[re] located down what was known as t[he] Vinegar Branch, and the compa[ny] later became Heenan & Froude.
P. B. Whitehouse Collecti[on]

Plate 23: A cutting near Sutton Coldfield, photographed during the construction of the extension line to Lichfield where it met the old South Staffs Railway. The line was opened to Lichfield (City) Station on 15th December 1884, with intermediate stations at Four Oaks, where many suburban trains from Birmingham were to terminate, Blake Street and Shenstone.

City of Birmingham Public Libraries

Plate 24: A Webb 2-4-2 tank, carrying express head-lamps, stands at Llandrindod Wells with a through coach to Birmingham (New Street) in 1899. The engine number is not readable, but in a photograph taken two years earlier at the same station 2-4-2 tank No. 93¹ was portrayed. Note the fireman with the single line staff, which is to be exchanged with the signalman at the box on the immediate left of the photograph. In pre-1914 days, as many as five through coaches a day made this journey to and from Swansea.

Warwick County Record Office

Plate 25 (above): The Midland goods yard at Lawley Street, cir[c]
1895. Apart from private-owner wagons, the majority seem to [be]
carrying the Midland Railway's initials. However, in the l[e]
foreground is an unusual vehicle, this being one from the Ca[m]
brian Railways, complete with Prince of Wales' feathers crest.
the centre background is Saltley Shed and to its left, the Saltl[ey]
Gasworks of the City of Birmingham.

Crown Copyright, National Railway Museu[m]

Plate 26 (left): Two Tyseley worthies from around the century[']
turn—an Inspector and Sub-Inspector from the Signal & T[ele]
graph Department of the GWR. *Warwick County Museu[m]*

Plate 27 (Right upper): At the end of the last century the Midla[nd]
Railway, like several other companies, found itself with great[ly]
increased traffic and a shortage of locomotive power. With th[eir]
own workshops and those of other private manufacturers in t[he]
middle of a boom in construction, the Midland turned [to]
America in the form of the Baldwin Locomotive Works and t[he]
Schenectady Locomotive Works, and they supplied kits for thir[ty]
and ten locomotives respectively in 1899. This photograph sho[ws]
Baldwin No. 16631 in course of erection *outside* the Derby Wor[ks]
building. The Baldwin engines worked out of Toton and hence [to]
Washwood Heath yard. Although Derby cannot be said to be [in]
the West Midlands, the picture is included here because of [its]
particular interest, and the fact that Birmingham was one of t[he]
few cities to see these engines. They were all withdrawn by 191[?].

P. B. Whitehouse Collecti[on]

Plate 28 (right lower): Great Western 2-4-0 locomotive No. 2[?]
with a local train for Evesham and beyond, stands in the 'u[p'
platform at Worcester sometime between 1893 and 1904. T[he]
engine (West Midland Railway No. 102) was built by Bey[er]
Peacock as a 2-2-2 (Works No. 247) in 1861, and was renewed [by]
the GWR as a 2-4-0 in 1883, finally being withdrawn in M[ay]
1920. *P. B. Whitehouse Collecti[on]*

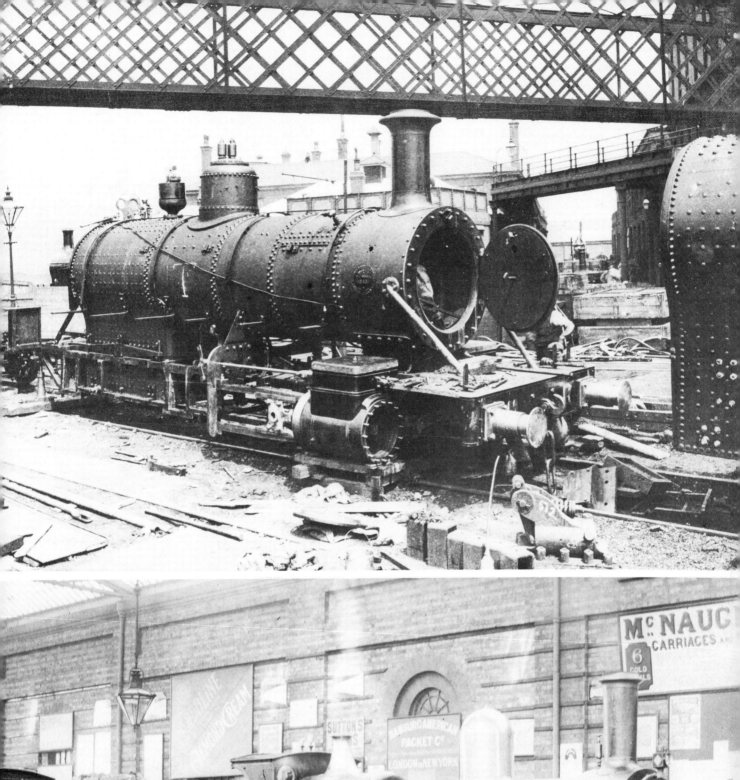

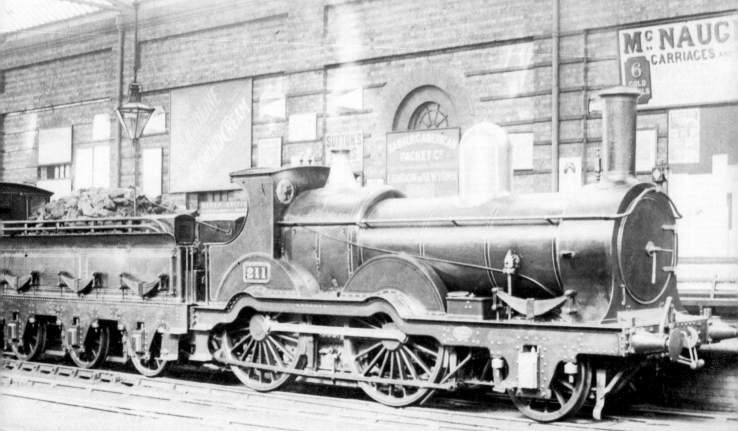

Wetton Mill Station, Manifold Valley, North Stafford Railway.

Plates 29 & 30: Scenes from official Leek & Manifold Railway postcards, circa 1907. Note the wording North Stafford Railway at the bottom of two of the pictures. The line was 2 ft. 6 in. gauge, and ran between Waterhouses (where it met the North Stafford Railway) and Hulme End. In their excellent book on the railway, the authors ("Manifold") quote the opinion of one of the navvies. 'It's a grand bit of line, but they wunna make a go on it for it starts from nowhere and finishes up at same place.' He was right.

Ian Wright Collection

Plate 31 (above): Coleshill station on the Hampton to Whitacre line circa 1905 (see dot on signal arm). Note the two platform levels and the wooden sign prominently erected at the platform end. It reads Gentlemen. Enamel signs on the platform include Sketchleys dry cleaning, EPPSS Cocoa, Millenium bread, Crossleys gas and oil engines plus a poster advertising holiday accommodation. The home signal is presumably protecting the level crossing in the foreground. Note the row of fire buckets adjacent to the toilets.

Warwick County Museum

Plates 32–34: Three photographs (two overleaf) showing construction of the Birmingham & North Warwickshire Railway in 1906. This line opened in 1908, and ran from a junction at Tyseley, on the GWR's Snow Hill to Leamington line, to Bearley where it linked up with the railway's Hatton to Stratford-upon-Avon branch.

City of Birmingham Public Libraries

Plate 35: **A July 1911 view of a double-headed train breasting the summit of the Lickey Incline. Although the rear of the train** is shrouded in what seems to be mist, this is more likely to have been steam from the train engine which is a Class 1P 2-4-0 locomotive. The pilot engine is Class 3P 4-4-0 No. 779.

Crown Copyright, National Railway Museum

Plate 36: A pre-World War I photograph of a 'down' express passing Halesowen Junction, behind a saturated Johnson Class 2P, 4-4-0 rebuilt with a Deeley class H boiler.

W. Leslie Good, P. B. Whitehouse Collection

Plate 37: A pre-1914 photograph of Midla[n] Class 3P 4-4-0 No. 755, in original conditi[on] and immaculately clean, heading a 'dow[n] train between Kings Norton and Northfie[ld] on the old four track section. Note the hors[e] box, which was still a familiar sight on pa[s]senger trains of that period, and the ne[w] train of clerestory stock.

P. B. Whitehouse Collecti[on]

Plate 38: Just as Cadburys provided the Midland Railway with considerable freight traffic to the south-west of Birmingham, so Burton-upon-Trent to the north-east abounded with brewery gold. The Burton-upon-Trent breweries had their own railway systems where trains were made up for collection, and the picture shows Allsopps Cooperage sidings and their locomotive No. 5. This was an 0-4-0ST built by Hudswell, Clarke & Rogers of Leeds (Works No. 177) in 1876, being scrapped in 1922.

P. B. Whitehouse Collection

Plate 39: The Preserved 'Spinner' Midland Railway No. 673 (one of the 1[?] p.s.i. boiler pressure 4-2-2s) of Johnson's 1887–99 batch heads an 'up' Der[by] bound express at Tamworth (High Level) on an unknown date. This engi[ne] was the last to remain in service, being withdrawn as late as 1928. No. 67[3] managed to escape the Stanier holocaust of Derby preserved engines and no[w] belongs to the National Collection where it carries the original number, 118.

W. Leslie Good, P. B. Whitehouse Collecti[on]

Plate 40: This photograph, taken at the west end of Derby Station, is included for its subject matter in the form of a North Stafford Railway train. The locomotive, NSR No. 1, is an 0-6-2 tank designed by Adams but actually built in 1923, and it is interesting to note that in spite of this, it carries full North Stafford Railway livery.

W. Leslie Good, P. B. Whitehouse Collection

Plate 41: A Malvern and Worcester to Paddington express at Moreton-in-Marsh, headed by GWR 'Bulldog' class 4-4-0 No. 3446 Goldfinch. This locomotive was built in November 1909 as No. 3736 and scrapped in 1948. The photograph is just out of period, being taken on 24th April 1923.

H. G. W. Household

Birmingham (New Street) Station

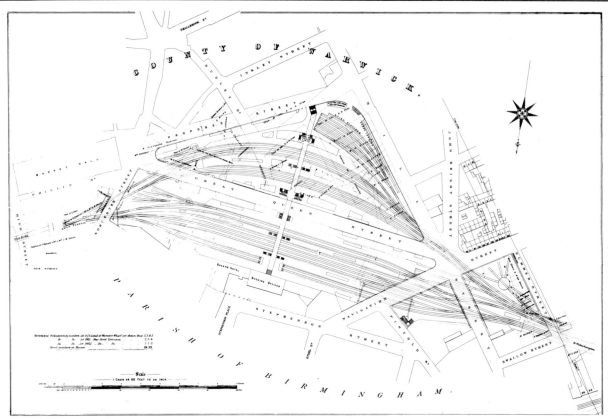

The London & Birmingham Railway set up its northern terminus at Curzon Street in the form of a 'mini' Euston, with the first trains running into it during April 1838. Later, in 1841, the Birmingham & Gloucester Railway made a junction with the London & Birmingham, and obtained running powers into its station thus bringing two companies into Curzon Street. Meanwhile, the Stour Valley line had been authorised in 1846, including a proposed central terminus in Birmingham fronting Navigation Street, the name by which the station was first known. This was opened in 1852 as a temporary platform.

By 1846, the London & Birmingham Railway had amalgamated with the Grand Junction Railway, whose original terminus was at Vauxhall, to form the London & North Western Railway. Meanwhile, the Birmingham & Derby Junction Railay had joined with the North Midland and Midland Counties railways to form the Midland Railway which, in its turn, absorbed the then Bristol & Birmingham line. The end result of company bargaining was that an agreement was reached for a large new station to be built, with LNWR ownership and Midland Railway participation at a nominal rent, plus a contribution to working expenses. This station butted on to the Stour Valley platform, thus giving through running to the north-west. Navigation Street Station (soon to be called New Street) was opened on 1st June 1854, with Midland Railway participation starting on 1st July. The station served LNWR trains running north over the Grand Junction route via Bescot and Wolverhampton, and south to London via Coventry and Rugby, with running arrangements over the Stour Valley line to Wolverhampton. On the Midland Railway trains ran northeast to Derby, and south-west via the Camp Hill line to Cheltenham, Gloucester and Bristol.

As traffic grew and the companies prospered, it soon became obvious that the station should be enlarged considerably. This was done by acquiring land on the south side taking in the thoroughfare known as Great Queen Street. This became a central drive and the new station was constructed beyond it. The work was mooted in 1880, put in hand in 1882 and completed in 1885. The opening was in 1885, from which date the Midland Railway took possession of the new section as a matter of convenience. A great improvement from the Midland's point of view was their ability to run trains through from Derby to Bristol without reversing back up the Camp Hill line, achieved by their acquisition of the Birmingham West Suburban Railway in 1875. This was built by private promoters and opened on 3rd April 1876; and ran from a junction with the Midland Railway between Lifford and Kings Norton, to a terminus at Granville Street. But it was diverted and extended to New Street via a series of tunnels, in time for the 1885 opening.

Increasing traffic caused other problems as the lines from Coventry, Gloucester, Derby and Aston all met within a quarter of a mile or so of each other. Congestion in this

Plates 42 & 43 (right upper and lower): Two drawings from the *Illustrated London News* of 3rd June 1854 showing the Stephenson Street exterior (including Queens Hotel above) of the Grand Central Station, later New Street, and the interior looking from the east. At the time the station was a dead end for Midland Railway trains (seen on the right) although from 1852, trains worked from a platform to the west of the station over the Stour Valley line to Wolverhampton.

Millbrook House Collection

The drawings reproduced from the *Illustrated London News* of 3rd June 1854 appeared with the following text:

NEW GRAND CENTRAL RAILWAY STATION AT BIRMINGHAM

The progressive extension of the railway system has led to the erection of several buildings for its general purposes; and these structures are entitled to rank amongst the most stupendous architectural works of the age. It is true that a certain critic of the day has sneered at the general taste displayed in our railway edifices, and the designs of engineers may not be sufficiently ornate for the architect's standard; nevertheless, the combined genius of both professions to meet our railway requirements have produced some striking results; and the London and North-Western Company, as the proprietors of the largest railway in the kingdom, have just added to their building a station of corresponding magnitude; erected for the accommodation of their own immense traffic and that of the Midland, Stour Valley, and North Staffordshire lines. This grand Central Station, which was opened on Thursday last, June 1st, is situated in New Street, Birmingham. The entrance is at the bottom of Stephenson-place, where is a plain gateway leading to the main front of the station and hotel, which we shall describe more fully and illustrate next week. Entering the Station by an arcade, we arrive at the booking-offices for the respective railways; and, passing through these, emerge on a magnificent corridor or gallery, guarded by a light railing, and open to the Station (but enclosed by the immense glass and iron roof), from whence broad stone staircases, with bronze rails, afford access to the departure platform. We then stand on a level with a long series of offices, appropriated to the officials of the Companies; and a superb refreshment room, about eighty feet long by forty broad, divided into three portions by rows of massive pillars.

We have now reached the interior of the Station, which our Artist (Mr. J. M. Williams) has so accurately and effectively represented upon the preceding page; and the details of which we abridge from Aris's Birmingham Gazette:

We must ask the reader to imagine that he stands on a stone platform, a quarter of a mile long; that behind him is a range of forty-five massive pillars projecting from the Station wall; that in front of him are ten lines of railways, four platforms, and a broad carriage-way, bounded by another range of forty-five massive iron pillars; and that, above all this, there stretches from pillar to pillar, a semicircular roof, 1100 feet long, 205 feet wide, and 80 feet high, composed of iron and glass, without the slightest support except that afforded by the pillars on either side. Let him add to this, that he stands on a stone platform a quarter of a mile long, amidst the noise of half a dozen trains arriving or departing, the trampling of crowds of passengers, the transport of luggage, the ringing of bells, and the noise of two or three hundred porters and workmen, and he will have a faint idea of the scene witnessed daily at the Birmingham Central Railway Station.

The roof merits more particular description. It consists of 36 principals or arches of iron strongly framed together. The upper bar, which is called a rib is curved in the segment of a circle; and each end rests upon a pillar; but between the rib and the pillar an ingenious system of rollers is introduced, so as to allow of either expansion or contraction by atmospheric changes. From each rib depend, at regular intervals, twelve 'struts' which are laced together by diagonal bars. The lower ends of the struts are attached to a bar or iron called the tie-rod; and which corresponds in curvature with the rib. Each of these principals weighs about 25 tons. They are placed at intervals of 24 feet from each other. Each rib is composed of five distinct pieces, riveted together. These ponderous metal bars were raised by means of a travelling stage; and the last rib was fixed on the anniversary of the day when the first pillar was set up. The pillars weigh 3 tons 12 cwt each. From rib to rib numerous 'purlins' are stretched, and these serve to support the smaller divisions of the glazed roof. The roof is composed of glass and corrugated iron—the former bearing a proportion of three-fourths to the latter, which runs along in a broad strip on each side, and in two bands on the crown of the arches.

The ends of the station, both at Worcester-street and Navigation-street, are screened off down to the tie-rods with glass. It is proposed, we understand, to continue the roof to Navigation-street-bridge, but the continuation will be ridge-and-furrow, like the Great Exhibition of 1851. We must not omit to notice that ample provision is made for ventilation, by raising a lantern over the centre bay of the principals, and continuing it down the whole length of the roof. An elegant iron bridge crosses the station from the booking-offices' corridor, and affords passengers a safe and efficient means of reaching the further platforms by flights of steps descending from the bridge.

Plate 44: The diverted Birmingham & Derby line, passing under the London & Birmingham tracks from New Street Coventry, is shown with the remains of the old connecting viaduct on the right. The date of the photograph is 18th August 194* J. C. Flemmons, P. B. Whitehouse Collection

bottleneck became almost unmanageable while fog, bad weather and extra holiday trains enlarged the problem. Salvation came with an agreement between the companies to widen the east tunnel, to lay down two additional tracks between Gloucester Junction and New Street, diverting the Derby line to take it under the London & Birmingham Railway to the south side and extending the Gloucester tracks to join it close to the new section in May 1896. Three years later the intersection, on the line between the old London & Birmingham and Grand Junction lines at Curzon Street, was abolished, by carrying the latter over the now goods only lines by a viaduct.

Because of the enormity of the works and their relevant costs, the Midland paid its share and in consequence, whilst New Street remained LNWR property, it became a joint station, for all practical purposes, from 1897. As a result, the station superintendent alternated between LNWR and Midland Railway nominees.

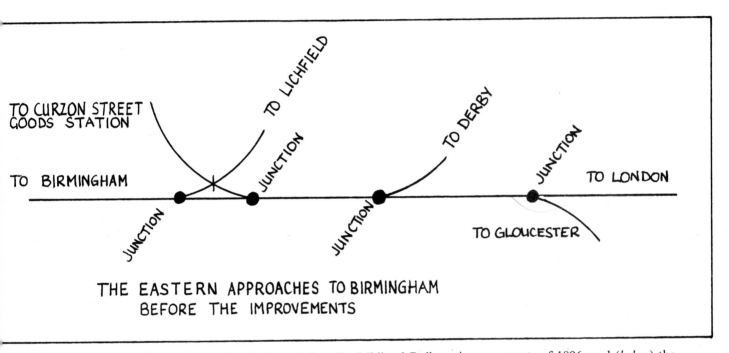

THE EASTERN APPROACHES TO BIRMINGHAM
BEFORE THE IMPROVEMENTS

Above: The eastern approaches to Birmingham before the Midland Railway improvements of 1896; and (*below*) the restructured approaches upon completion of the improvements and the abolition in 1899 of the Curzon Street intersection.

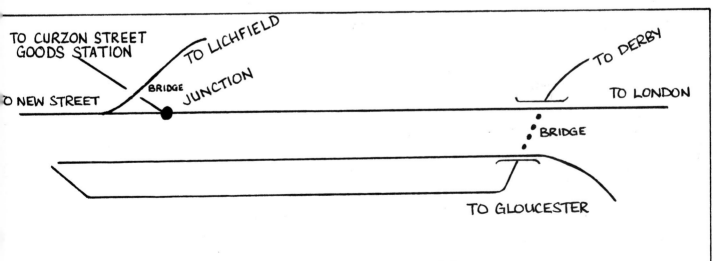

THE EASTERN APPROACHES TO BIRMINGHAM
AFTER THE IMPROVEMENTS

One of the striking features of New Street Station was its footbridge, probably one of the busiest thoroughfares in the then City of Birmingham. When, in 1846, powers were granted by Parliament for the station to be built, it was appreciated that it would absorb a large area of land within the city centre, involving a long detour by foot between two busy neighbourhoods. Accordingly, a special provision obliged the LNWR to provide and maintain a footbridge for public use. In the event, this was so built that it provided the only access to the platforms, but also ensured that New Street became an 'open' station, necessitating ticket collection on all local trains at the suburban station prior to its entry.

During the late nineteenth century, New Street Station was performing a social service in the city by acting as a meeting place and centre of life. Sometimes, according to contemporary reports, Saturday nights were marred by 'young bloods' who, after closing time, would come to New Street and book to Monument Lane (the first station beyond the tunnel and a penny fare). This made them genuine travellers in the eyes of the law, and entitled them to further drinks in the refreshment rooms.

Full details of the station and its workings, plus the suburban and main line destinations of its trains, can easily be obtained by reading the copies of the *Railway Magazine* for April 1900 and November 1915 respectively. The complications of traffic dealt with at New Street can clearly be seen by checking an hour's departures during the rush-hour period between 5.00 and 6.00 p.m., taken from the November issue and reproduced below. Arrivals, naturally, were similarly comprehensive.

	Time	Destination	Platform
L.N.W.	5.0	Stafford (Thursdays only)	3 Bay
L.N.W.	5.0	London	1 Main Up
MID.	5.0	Redditch, Evesham and Aschchurch (via South-West Surburban line)	5 Down
L.N.W.	5.5	Sutton Coldfield and Four Oaks	2 Up
L.N.W.	5.5	Wolverhampton	2 Up
MID.	5.6	King's Norton (via Camp Hill)	4 Up
L.N.W.	5.8	Hampton	1 (2 South Stafford Bay)
L.N.W.	5.12	Empties of train from North in at 5.5	1 Main Up
MID.	5.14	Nuneaton, Leicester, London King's Lynn	5 Up
MID.	5.15	Worcester, Ashchurch, Malvern and Bristol slow	6 Down
L.N.W.	5.15	Harborne	1 (2 Stour Valley Bay)
L.N.W.	5.15	Sutton Coldfield and Four Oaks	2 Up
MID.	5.20	King's Norton (via West Suburban line)	6 Bay
L.N.W.	5.25	Wolverhampton	3 Down
L.N.W.	5.30	Walsall, Rugeley, Lichfield Via Soho Road)	2 Down
L.N.W.	5.30	Cocentry and London	1 (1 South Stafford Bay)
MID.	5.30	Walsall and Wolverhampton	4 Up
L.N.W.	5.35	Harborne	1 (1 Stour Valley Bay)
L.N.W.	5.37	Sutton Coldfield	2 Up
MID.	5.38	Circle Train outward, Via Camp Hill	5 Up
L.N.W.	5.40	Walsall and Wolverhampton (via Soho Road)	2 Down
L.N.W.	5.40	Leamington	1 (2 South Stafford Bay)
MID.	5.40	Cheltenham, Gloucester and Bristol	6 Down
MID.	5.42	Burton, Derby, Bradford and N.W. line	4 Up
L.N.W.	5.43	Coventry and Leamington	1 Main Up
MID.	5.48	Tamworth, Burton and N.E. line (Mondays, Fridays and Saturdays) only	4 Up
L.N.W.	5.50	Walsall)via Aston)	1 Main Up
L.N.W.	5.50	Liverpool, Leeds and Manchester	3 Down
MID.	5.50	Gloucester slow	5 Down
MID.	5.55	Tamworth and Nuneaton slow	5 Up
L.N.W.	6.0	Harborne	1 (1 Stour Valley Bay)
L.N.W.	6.0	Sutton Coldfield, Lichfield, Burton, Derby	1 (1 South Stafford Bay)

As completed, the station had six platforms (island platforms counting as one) and several bays. Platforms 1, 2 and 3 comprised the old North Western Railway side and 4, 5 and 6 the Midland Railway side. This confusing numbering, with platform 2 facing platform 3 and platform 5 facing platform 4, etc., persisted until the end of LMS days.

Plate 46 (below): Platform No. 1, the main 'down' platform, pictured in 1885. On the left the close coupled coaching stock shows a remarkable lineage from the stage coach, and is still using oil lamps. The legends on the door panels read first smoking, second smoking, third smoking and third respectively. The time exposure shows a ghostly figure leaving the train whilst in the background are beautifully strapped and belted LNWR guards. The footbridge signal is over their heads, while two signalmen stand chatting outside their cabin just above the train. This photograph is of particular interest because it must have been deliberately taken around February 8th 1885, when the new Midland Railway platforms were taken into use. On the right are Midland coaches, and the train indicator board pointing to platform 1B reads Midland trains to Worcester Gloster (sic) and Bristol. Advertisements include (over the arch) National Provincial for patent medicines, Russells Watches of Church Street Liverpool, Barrows New Stores and Anglo Bavarian Ales, whilst the posters below include the magazine *Truth* and the *Girl's Own Paper*. The lettering over platforms B and A reads South Stafford Bay. The two trains on the left are probably the 3.10 p.m. to Leamington via Coventry (see destination boards on coaches) and, behind the brake third, the 3.35 p.m. to Hampton. *Millbrook House Collection*

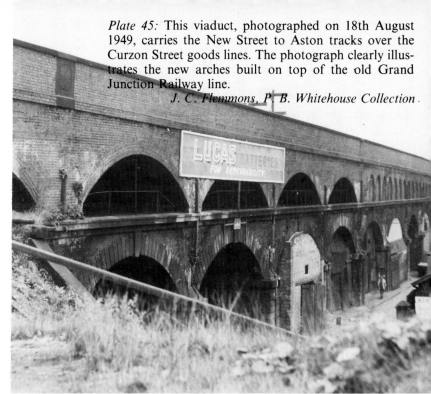

Plate 45: This viaduct, photographed on 18th August 1949, carries the New Street to Aston tracks over the Curzon Street goods lines. The photograph clearly illustrates the new arches built on top of the old Grand Junction Railway line.

J. C. Flemmons, P. B. Whitehouse Collection

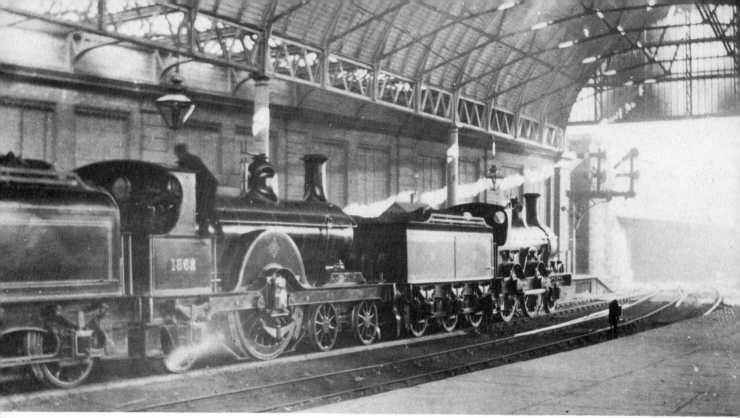

Plate 47: **A double-headed train** for Derby (or beyond) stand alongside platform 4, at New Street Station, (Midland side circa 1900. Note the early diamond pattern crest on the splasher of No. 1862, Queen Drive Bridge in the background and the LNWR signals controlled by No. 2 signal box on platform 5 just off the picture to the right.

Warwick County Office

Plate 48: Ramsbottom 0-6-0 saddle tank No. 3202, as rebuilt by Francis Webb but still with no overall cab, stands as south end pilot at New Street Station in 1902. Even though the engine would have been used to shunt passenger stock, it is interesting to note that it still carries no continuous brake, merely a three link coupling. Note the sparse and simple cab fittings with no vacuum brake fitted and also that all pipework is burnished as are the regulator handle and spectacle plates. The shed plate 10 (Aston) is clearly seen at the top of the front weather plate. No. 3202 must have been nearing the end of its life, although still outwardly shining and cared for, as by October 1909, a DX goods engine built in 1865, was carrying No. 3202.

Warwick County Office

Plate 49: The frontage of the LNWR Queens Hotel in August 1904. The main entrance to New Street Station is beneath the arcade in the centre of the picture. This scene was to remain virtually unchanged for another half century. The excursion poster in the foreground announces day trips to Pwllheli on the Cambrian Coast, via Bangor and Afon Wen Junction.

Crown Copyright, National Railway Museum

Plate 50: A Webb 18 in. 0-6-2 tank built in May 1893 heads a local train to Sutton Coldfield circa 1905. These engines worked the Lichfield line local services well into the 1930s, when they were replaced by the Stanier 2-6-4 tanks.

P. B. Whitehouse Collection

Plates 51 & 52: Two of Webb's 6 ft 6 in. 'Precedent' class 2-4-0 locomotives stand in New Street, the exact date being unknown although it is prior to 1907. They are No. 865 *Envoy* built in 1877, rebuilt in 1894 and lasting into LMS days and No. 2181 *Buffalo*, built in 1874/5 and withdrawn before 1907, when 'Precursor' class *Eleanor* took that number

P. B. Whitehouse Collection

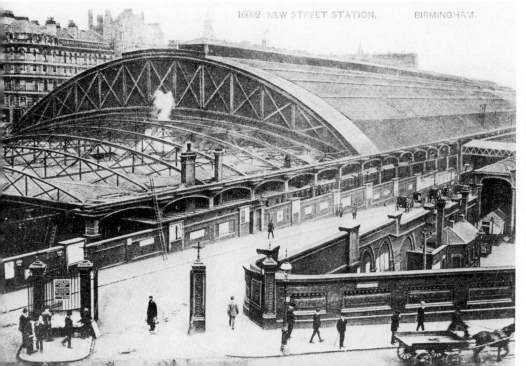

16002 NEW STREET STATION. BIRMINGHAM.

Plate 53: A pre-1907 postcard view of the LNWR side of New Street Station looking down Queens Drive. The cast iron notice attached to the railings in the foreground indicates that the latter is a private road, and that person found trespassing there or on the station will be prosecuted. Note the Hansom cabs lined up adjacent to the old platform No. 3, and the steam tram track from John Bright Street to High Street in the right foreground. The initials LMS were marked on the car by a small boy in the 1930s!

P. B. Whitehouse Collection

The first is a view taken from the east end, showing the horse-box bay running off platform No. 3. This platform served 'down' expresses and to the end of the station, the length of this platform proved extremely short, often requiring trains to draw forward. In the centre is the island platform No. 2, used mainly for suburban traffic whilst on the right, two Webb 4 ft. 6 in. passenger 2-4-2 tanks stand adjacent to Platform No. 1. To the right of these engines is No. 1 bay, with the Queens Hotel building behind. In the distance is the footbridge which gave access from Stephenson Street (the station did not serve New Street!). It ran on to Queens Drive, across the Midland Railway section to Station Street. *P. B. Whitehouse Collection*

…his slightly closer view shows a shunting …orse in the foreground, and some of the later …rancis Webb's passenger tanks to the right. …he original negative was probably slightly …nder exposed, as an artist has touched in the …heels and added coupling/connecting rods …f his own design.

P. B. Whitehouse Collection

…elow) This last view is closer still and shows …atform No. 3 in more detail. The short train … the left is pulled right up to the bracket …nal but not quite beyond the footbridge …nal, which can just be seen above and to … left of the rear vehicle. On platform No. 2, … train indicator, with its hand clocks, …nds close to the bottom of the steps.

P. B. Whitehouse Collection

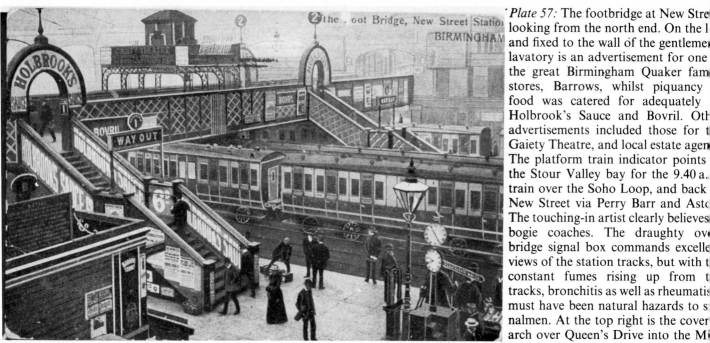

Plate 57: The footbridge at New Stre[et] looking from the north end. On the l[eft] and fixed to the wall of the gentleme[n's] lavatory is an advertisement for one [of] the great Birmingham Quaker fam[ily] stores, Barrows, whilst piquancy [in] food was catered for adequately [by] Holbrook's Sauce and Bovril. Oth[er] advertisements included those for t[he] Gaiety Theatre, and local estate agen[ts]. The platform train indicator points [to] the Stour Valley bay for the 9.40 a.[m.] train over the Soho Loop, and back [to] New Street via Perry Barr and Ast[on]. The touching-in artist clearly believes [in] bogie coaches. The draughty ov[er] bridge signal box commands excelle[nt] views of the station tracks, but with t[he] constant fumes rising up from t[he] tracks, bronchitis as well as rheumatis[m] must have been natural hazards to s[ig]nalmen. At the top right is the cover[ed] arch over Queen's Drive into the Mi[d]land Railway station, with shops to t[he] left and right.

P. B. Whitehouse Collect[ion]

Plate 58: A photograph taken circa 1910, showing a typical crowd crossing the New Street Station footbridge and indicating that even in the early afternoon, around 2.35 p.m., it was thronged with people, most of whom were not using the station. The picture was taken from the steps coming down from the LNWR booking hall and looking towards the Midland Railway side. Even some fifty years after its construction, the glass roof was clean and the station well lit. Advertisements include Priory Tea, Barrows Al Stores, Bird's Custard, Nestle's Purest Swiss Milk, Coleman's Mustard and Dare's Premier Ales at 2/- per doz. (large), delivered weekly.

P. B. Whitehouse Collection

Plate 59: Rare enough in any event the appearance of a Derby-erected American Mogul in New Street was something to be remembered. In 1898, to act as stop gaps to help cope with ever-mounting traffic, the Midland Railway acquired forty of these engines including thirty from Baldwin and ten from the Schenectady Locomotive Works. They had short lives and No. 2233, shown here with an empty stock working between platforms 5 and 6, was the last survivor, being withdrawn in 1915.

W. Leslie Good, P. B. Whitehouse Collection

Plate 60: On the left is Webb's 'Precedent' class 2-4-0 No. 514 *Puck* (*Lawrence* until May 1913), with tender coaled up but still carrying a light engine headlamp. The engine carries its older type buffers and dates from 1880, although it was rebuilt in December 1895. The express on the right in platform 3 is headed by an unknown Precursor, which may have been No. 7 *Titan* or No. 1573 *Dunrobin*, both of which were fairly regular performers into New Street. The photograph is dated around 1920/1.

W. Leslie Good, P. B. Whitehouse Collection

Plate 61: One of the wartime-built 'Prince of Wales' class 4-6-0s No. 95 *Gallipoli* (March 1916) is seen in almost pristine external condition as it blows off prior to moving off with what was probably a Grand Junction routed express to the north.

W. Leslie Good, P. B. Whitehouse Collection

Plate 62: A 'Prince of Wales' class 4-6-0 with an indecipherable number ending in 4, waits with a train of empty stock on the through line between platforms 2 and 1 at New Street, in the later days of the LNWR. As the tender is fully coaled, it seems likely that the engine has come down from Aston Shed ready to work its train to the north via Wolverhampton.

A. W. Flower

Plate 63: Webb 18 in. 0-6-2 tank, No. 775 of 1902 (with 5 ft 0 in driving wheels) with local train headlamp, waits between platforms 1 and 2 around 1921. Note the still clean glass in the station roof.

A. W. Flowers

Plate 64: A comparatively rare view of a Webb four cylinder Compound in New Street, very much in its declining years. 'Alfred the Great' class No. 1974 *Howe*, built in August 1903, was the only one of its class to be superheated (in May 1921) and ran with its LNWR number until it was scrapped in 1928. The LMS number allocated was 5128.

A. W. Flowers

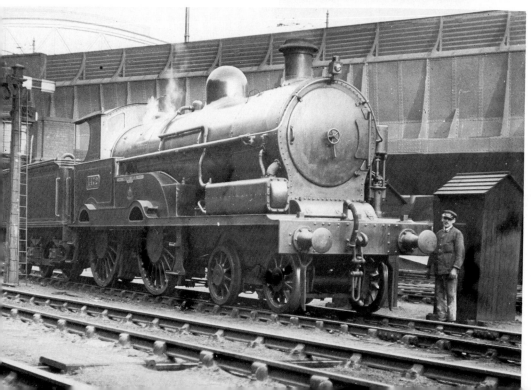

Plate 65: 'George the Fifth' class No. 1472 *Moor Hen*, complete with experimental feed water heater, waits to pick up a north-bound local train to Wolverhampton and Stafford circa 1920. The photograph is taken from the west end of the long Stour Valley bay, a favourite spot for locomotive watchers as from here, one could also see the Midland trains running in and out of platforms 4, 5 and 6.

W. Leslie Good, P. B. Whitehouse Collection

Plate 66: The West end station pilot in 1920 was Webb 2-4-2 tank No. 1389. In later days, the class was generally superseded on this duty by an 18 in. 0-6-2 tank.

W. Leslie Good, P. B. Whitehouse Collection

Plate 67: Bowen–Cooke 'George the Fifth' class 4-4-0 No. 1713 *Partridge* stands beyond the Navigation Street Bridge, at the west end of the station, just before the Grouping. Note the fireman relaxing with his newspaper, the generally poor quality of the coal, the large capuchon to the chimney (similar to a Webb Compound) and the left-hand buffer beam lamp in, to say the least, an unusual position.

W. Leslie Good, P. B. Whitehouse Collection

Plate 68: New Street on a sunny day. One of the Euston to Birmingham, Dudley Port and Wolverhampton expresses, headed by a 'George the Fifth' class 4-4-0, rolls into platform 3 through the smoke and shafts of sunlight. This photograph, taken in the early 1920s, shows New Street very much as it appeared to the normal traveller at that time, seemingly dark and somewhat murky but full of character. The photograph was taken from the east end of platform 3.

Eric Griffiths FRPS, Courtesy Kodak Ltd.

Plate 69: Right from the establishment of the Midland Railway side of New Street in 1885, and the consequent through running via the old Birmingham West Suburban line, north-west expresses used this section. This photograph, taken during the last years of the pre-grouping era, shows a rare appearance of a 'Claughton' in the station. No. 2204 *Sir Herbert Walker KCB*, almost certainly from Shed 26 (Edge Hill) is seen with a noon arrival of the 'Pines Express' from Liverpool. The train was more frequently worked by an Edge Hill 'Prince of Wales' or 'George the Fifth' locomotive but its arrival, usually as Big Brum (the Council House clock—a paler imitation of Big Ben) was striking 12, was always a matter of interest as the train swung across west of the LNWR North Tunnel, to pass in front of No. 5 signal box, and come to a stand at a Midland platform—usually No. 4 as seen here. Note the destboards headed Snowdon Mountain Railway and M & SWJR.*W. Leslie Good, P. B. Whitehouse Collection*

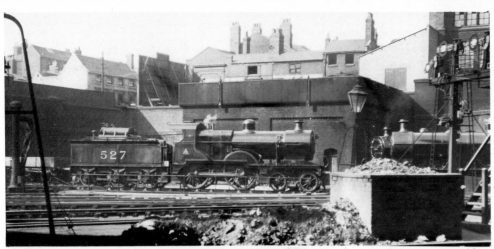

Plate 70: Two superheated Midland Cla[ss] 2P 4-4-0 locomotives at the west end of t[he] station, circa 1920, alongside a still satu[r]ated version of the class. Oil-burning N[o.] 527 sits on the turntable whilst No. 5[42] stands in the background behind her uns[u]perheated sister, possibly No. 368 or 36[9.] The New Street turntable was very sma[ll] being unhappy with anything larger than [a] 4-4-0 or a 0-6-0.
W. Leslie Good, P. B. Whitehouse Colle[c]ti[on]

Plate 71: Resplendent in Midland Re[d] Class 2 No. 542 from Shed 10 (Leiceste[r)] waits alongside platform 5 with a homew[]ard-bound local train. This platform w[as] used for stopping trains, either east or we[st] bound, at will. No. 542 was one of the lat[e] (1901) batch of engines to be superheat[ed] by Fowler after 1912. The first engine to [be] withdrawn was not until Nationalisatio[n.] *W. Leslie Good, P. B. Whitehouse Colle[c]ti[on]*

Plate 72: The first of Kirtley's 800 class [of] 1870/1, No. 24, stands out beyond pla[t]form 4 whilst on station pilot duties in t[he] Midland side of New Street, circa 1922.
A. W. Flowe[r]

Lines South-West from New Street

Originally, the Midland Railway had access to Birmingham from the south-west by virtue of the old Birmingham & Gloucester line, which came in from Kings Norton and Lifford via Camp Hill, making a junction with the London & Birmingham line near Curzon Street. Even after the completion of New Street station in 1854, trains from Derby still reversed to continue their journeys in the Gloucester direction.

The Birmingham & Gloucester Railway was opened from Cheltenham to Bromsgrove on 24th June 1840, followed by an extension north to a temporary platform at Cofton Farm on 17th September of that year. Its stations included Blackwell, at the summit of the notorious Lickey Incline, and Barnt Green.

By 17th December, a further section was opened with stations at Longbridge, Lifford, Moseley and Camp Hill. Trains ran into Curzon Street on 17th August 1841, Camp Hill then becoming a goods station.

The year 1871 saw the authorisation of the Birmingham West Suburban Railway, with the actual opening taking place in 1876 and, throughout its life, this probably underwent more changes than any other line in the district. At first, it was intended to be no more than a single track, stretching from a junction with the Midland Railway at Lifford to a central terminus at Albion Wharf. But eventually, it was cut back to Granville Street having, in the interim, become part of the Midland Railway. There were four stations, these being at Stirchley Street, Selly Oak, Somerset Road and Church Road (Stirchley Street being renamed Stirchley Street & Bournville on 4th March 1880, renamed Bournville & Stirchley Street in July 1888 and finally, Bournville in April 1904). Lifford Station was opened on 1st June 1876 but trains were worked into Kings Norton by the Midland Railway from 3rd April 1876, with doubling and a connection at Church Road (near Granville Street which was closed) to a new station at Five Ways completed in 1881. Trains ran through to New Street as from 1885. At the same time, the section between Church Road and Granville Street was extended to give access to the new Central Goods Depot opened close to Suffolk Street in 1897, this including tunnelling on a gradient of 1 in 80.

The completion of the Birmingham West Suburban line required a new junction at Lifford where the station was resited for the third time, and put back on the Old Birmingham & Gloucester line. The curve at Lifford was opened in 1864, whilst a triangle was completed there in 1892 to enable a circular suburban service to be initiated, running out one way from New Street and back the other.

A further outlet was opened on 10th September 1883 called the Halesowen Railway (Joint Midland and Great Western). Trains were run from Halesowen by the Midland Railway to Kings Norton with connections to Granville Street and on the completion of New Street, one morning and one evening train ran through.

Four Scenes on the old Birmingham & Gloucester section

Plate 73: Midland Railway Class 3 0-6-0 No. 3694 passes Brighton Road Station sometime between 1907 and 1909. This is a 'down' train of empty coaching stock, running from Birmingham (New Street) to Kings Norton carriage sidings. No. 21 is a reporting number and is unidentifiable, as the Midland did not use such numbers in the working timetable but only on high days and holidays, when they were in the weekly notices.

P. B. Whitehouse Collection

Plates 74–76: Three photographs of Moseley Station, taken on the Lifford Loop just outside the city. Note the short tunnel, built in this form to satisfy St. Mary's Church Authorities, under whose land the railway ran. The church is just discernible in the top right of the second photograph. The wooden bridge (looking towards Birmingham) carries what is now literally known as Woodbridge Road although this, and most other Birmingham & Gloucester Railway bridges were replaced by the Midland Railway in the early 1890s. The dates of the photographs appear to range around the 1870s when platform alterations were made. Note the later photograph, where strengthening pieces appear to have been added to the bridge.

City of Birmingham Public Libraries

**Four Scenes on the old Birmingham West
Suburban section**

City of Birmingham Public Libraries

Plate 77: One of S. W. Johnson's graceful engines of 1876 passes Somerset Road Station with an 'up' train, circa 1901. Note the lever frame on the 'down' platform, in use until closure of the station in 1929, controlling the home signal at the end of the platform and a relating distant signal. These signals were put to danger by the station staff on the arrival of a 'down' local train. No such frame existed on the 'up' platform.

The late Mrs A. Whitehouse

Plate 78: Midland Railway Kirtley do[u]-
ble-framed 2-4-0 No. 161A, with an 'u[p]
local at Somerset Road Station circa 19[0].
The engine was built at Derby in 1868 a[n]
renumbered 161A in August 1894, and it [is]
shown here as rebuilt in September 189[.]
In 1907, a further renumbering (17) to[ok]
place, and the locomotive was withdra[wn]
by the LMS in June 1928. Note that t[he]
original negative has long been lost a[nd]
that the print from it exposed in sunli[ght]
and sepia in tone, has lasted for well o[ver]
eighty years.

The late Mrs A. Whiteho[use]

Plate 79: An unknown Midland sin[gle]
approaches Somerset Road Station wit[h a]
'down' empty stock train, shortly bef[ore]
1907. Most of the vehicles appear to be [six]
wheelers, but at least 2 four-wheeled va[ns]
are in the consist. This must have be[en]
quite a performance for the locomoti[ve]
running out through the tunnels and c[ut]-
tings to Church Road Station and beyon[d].

P. B. Whitehouse Collecti[on]

Plate 80: Johnson 4-2-2 No. 76 approaches Somerset Road Station, with a 'down' express in 1907. The engine has its original Johnson chimney and boiler mountings, but the smokebox door is the flat Deeley type with lugs round the circumference. Its later number was 666; Deeley type numerals are on both the tender and smokebox door.

C. B. Harley, P. B. Whitehouse Collection

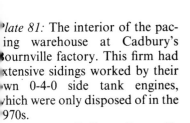

Plate 81: The interior of the packing warehouse at Cadbury's Bournville factory. This firm had extensive sidings worked by their own 0-4-0 side tank engines, which were only disposed of in the 1970s.

Cadbury, Bournville

Seven Scenes between King's Norton and Northfield

Plate 82: One of Deeley's 'hole in the wall' 0-6-4 tanks, No. 2027, complete with Saltley Shed Plate No. 3, takes a long train of empty stock over the 'down' goods line towards Northfield shortly before World War I. Note the lining on the front of the side tanks, and the LSWR and GC wagons in the background.

W. Leslie Good, P. B. Whitehouse Collection

Plate 83: The myth of 'M stands for Midland with engines galore—they have two on each train and keep asking for more' dies a death with this photograph, taken around 1921, of Johnson 6 ft. 6 in. 2-4-0 No. 164 at the head of eight bogies, albeit wooden non-corridor stock. The train, approaching Northfield, is probably a 'down' Worcester or Gloucester semi fast service. Note the destination board on the leading clerestory brake (there are three), which appears to read Worcester when examined under a glass.

W. Leslie Good, P. B. Whitehouse Collection

Plate 84: With a heavy load of eight bogies one of Johnson's 7 ft. 0 in. 1876–1880 design 2-4-0s, No. 206, carries Class A headlamps as she approaches Northfield, at the close of Midland Railway days. The train is probably a semi-fast service to Worcester, as the engine carries shed plate 4 on her smokebox door.

W. Leslie Good, P. B. Whitehouse Collection

Plate 85: Class 3P 4-4-0 No. 723, fitted with oil burning apparatus, nears Northfield with a 'down' fast train circa 1921. The leading vehicle is one of the magnificent six wheel bogie restaurant cars. The oil tanks in the tender seem to have been somewhat hastily installed, as they are too large for the coal space and lie askew.

W. Leslie Good, P. B. Whitehouse Collection

Plate 86: Another 6 ft. 9 in. 2-4-0 locomotive, again seen around 1921. In this picture, No. 244 leaves Kings Norton with a 'down' stopping train, made up of seven clerestories and a van.
W. Leslie Good, P. B. Whitehouse Collection

Plate 87: Two Midland 0-6-4 tanks, Nos. 2015 and 2039 with a 'down' empty stock train from Kings Norton, work over the fast line near Northfield around 1920. This is possibly an ECS train to Longbridge, where it would split into two portions for the return journeys to New Street, one via Camp Hill and the other via the Birmingham West Suburban line. Early evenings at Longbridge Station were interesting times for many years, with the Austin factory workers having their own trains over the Midland Railway to New Street, and GWR trains worked over the single line Halesowen Railway to Old Hill, giving connections to Dudley and Stourbridge.

W. Leslie Good, P. B. Whitehouse Collection

Plate 88: A scene at King's Norton Junction, circa 1921 taken before the widening. The train is a 'down' express, headed by Johnson superheated Class 2P No. 520 from Shed 3 (Saltley) with all clerestory stock including a non-corridor three coach set. The original signal box at King's Norton Junction can be seen on the far side of Pershore Road South Bridge.

W. Leslie Good, P. B. Whitehouse Collection

Three Scenes between Northfield and Halesowen Junction

Plate 89: An 'up' local train consisting of an elliptical roofed four coach set of bogie stock makes its way between Halesowen Junction and Northfield around 1920, behind the last of the Kirtley (rebuilt by Johnson) 2-4-0s to be constructed by Derby, No. 126. The class did not become extinct until 1938.

W. Leslie Good. P. B. Whitehouse Collection

Plate 90: Midland Class 3P 4-4-0 No. 777, with a 'down' Bristol express, passes under the gantry at Halesowen Junction. This is one of Leslie Good's very early photographs, as the signals still have circles on the back of the arms, and could be as early as 1910.

W. Leslie Good, P. B. Whitehouse Collection

Plate 91 (right): A 'down' express, between Northfield and Halesowen Junction circa 1920, headed by Kirtley (rebuilt by Johnson) Class 1P 2-4-0 No. 93, double-heading a saturated Class 2P 4-4-0. The pilot came from Saltley Shed (3), and the presumption would be that both engines came on the train at New Street. Ten coaches would have been considered too much for a non superheated 4-4-0.

W. Leslie Good, P. B. Whitehouse Collection

Six Scenes at Halesowen Junction

Plate 92: A Johnson high flyer, in th[e] form of 6 ft. 9 in. 2-4-0 No. 197, heads [a] 'down' semi fast train past Halesowe[n] Junction shortly before World War I.
W. Leslie Good, P. B. Whitehouse Co[l]lectio[n]

Plates 93 & 94 (below and right): Tw[o] photographs of Deeley 0-6-4 tank N[o.] 2015, having come to grief near Hale[sowen Junction, on the site of the ne[w] Longbridge Station, around 1921. Tw[o] of Saltley's steam cranes have bee[n] fetched out for the job, of note is th[e] Midland Railway coat of arms on th[e] small crane, and the use of outrigge[rs] on both. Possibly a combination of w[et] weather, spongy track and a class no[-] torious for its rolling all contributed t[o] the accident.
W. Leslie Good, P. B. Whitehouse Co[l]lectio[n]

Plate 97 (above): Halesowen Junction as pictured from the signal box, with Johnson 0-4-4 tank No. 1324 running bunker first with a local train, via the Camp Hill and Moseley line. From the appearance of mother and son watching from the embankment, the date must precede 1920. This was also prior to the start of widening, and this site is now occupied by the new Longbridge Station. Note the stacked coal in the bunker.

W. Leslie Good, P. B. Whitehouse Collection

Barnt Green

Plate 98 (below): Sometime around 1920, a through Ashchurch and Redditch train to Birmingham waits in the branch platform at Barnt Green, the junction with the main line to Worcester and Bristol. The Johnson 2-4-0, No. 176, is from Saltley Shed (3). Note the starter signal behind the footbridge, in an unusual position far back down the platform.

W. Leslie Good, P. B. Whitehouse Collection

Plate 95 (left top): Another photograph at Halesowen Junction, this time taken from the signal box and showing a train headed by one of the later Class 2P 4-4-0s, the superheated No. 526. Unfortunately the shed plate number is not decipherable.

W. Leslie Good, P. B. Whitehouse Collection

Plate 96 (left bottom): A 'down' express seen passing Halesowen Junction signal box, with Class 2P superheated 4-4-0 No. 405 from Shed 3 (Saltley) at its head. The engine is blowing off gently, as well as it should with its short five coach train. Note the name of the box, which appears to read 'Halesowen Main Line Junction'.

W. Leslie Good, P. B. Whitehouse Collection

The Lickey Incline

The Lickey Incline, between Blackwell and Bromsgrove, is one of the steepest gradients on any main line in Britain. Two miles at 1 in 37.7 was a heavy slog for any steam locomotive, particularly so from a standing start, so bankers were used on virtually every train, although the odd three coach passenger local did occasionally manage on its own. Bromsgrove shed maintained these engines, although inter-trip coaling and watering took place adjacent to the eastbound tracks. Engines used on this duty in Midland and LMS days were the standard 0-6-0 tanks and the mighty 'Big Bertha' or 'Big Emma', the 1920-built 0-10-0 locomotive specially constructed for the job. She was the largest engine ever to emerge from Derby works, and although trials were made by the LMS using other locomotives from time to time (including an ex-LNWR 0-8-4 tank), these never came to anything. Train loads were considered to be worth units of 0-6-0 tanks, and here the big banker was 'equal two'. It was not altogether uncommon to see a double-headed 0-6-0 freight train banked by three 0-6-0 tanks. A summer Saturday, with trains working block and block, was something to see and listen to right into the 1960s. All descending loose coupled freight workings had to stop at Blackwell for brakes to be pinned down.

Plate 99 (below): Smart in her Midland Railway livery and very clean, No. 2290, at the time Britain's only ten-coupled engine, stands at Blackwell Summit after dropping off a Birmingham bound train. The date is probably around 1920.
W. Leslie Good, P. B. White Collection

Plate 100: Banked by a single 0-6-0 tank, and with a train of seven coaches including a six wheel bogie diner, Class 2P 4-4-0 No. 525 breasts the summit of the bank at Blackwell circa 1920. For a change, it appears as if the train engine has been doing some hard work and the banker taking it more easily. Normally, the assisting locomotive worked hard, and shut off at the far end of the platform. No. 525 has been superheated, and comes from Saltley Shed (3).

W. Leslie Good, P. B. Whitehouse Collection

Plate 101: A double-headed 'down' express about to pass through Blackwell Station circa 1920, behind Johnson single wheeler No. 670 from Saltley Shed and an unknown superheated Class 2P 4-4-0. In the background is the newly-arrived 0-10-0 banker No. 2290. Note the absence of heating or brake hoses, and the unusual tender water capacity indicated by the plate which reads 2,050 gallons.

W. Leslie Good, P. B. Whitehouse Collection

Plate 102: Blackwell Station, at the summit of the incline, with two of Johnson's Class 2P 4-4-0 locomotives heading a 'down' train. The pilot has been superheated, whilst the train engine is still in saturated condition.

W. Leslie Good, P. B. Whitehouse Collection

Plate 103: A photograph taken from the north end of Blackwell 'down' platform circa 1920, with a Bristol-bound express behind Class 3P 4-4-0 No. 765, from Shed 1 (Derby), seen approaching on the main line. To the left is standard 0-6-0 tank No. 1954, and on the right an unknown Kirtley double-framed 2-4-0 with light engine headlamps. Note the cleanliness of the engines, as even the banker has its rear cab brass spectacle plates polished. This has just dropped off an 'up' train as it is still carrying a tail lamp, and the smoke of the departing train engine can be seen over the rear coaches of the express.

W. Leslie Good, P. B. Whitehouse Collection

Plate 104: Around 1920, No. 682 a Shed 8 (Bristol) Johnson single wheeler, double-heads a Class 2P 4-4-0 at the top of the Lickey Incline, with a 'down' Bristol express.

W. Leslie Good, P. B. Whitehouse Collection

Plate 105: Even though the load is only four bogies and a van, Class 3P 4-4-0 No. 715 makes heavy weather as it nears Blackwell with an 0-6-0 tank as the regulation banker. The engine carries a No. 7 Shed Plate (Gloucester). It was probably a spring afternoon photograph, as the sun has moved south-west making this more unusual view of an ascending train possible.

W. Leslie Good, P. B. Whitehouse Collection

Plate 106: **A Bristol-bound express, behind superheated Class 2P 4-4-0 No. 512, begins its descent down the incline around 1920. Note the relaid track, not yet properly ballasted.**

W. Leslie Good, P. B. Whitehouse Collection

Plate 107: Midland saturated Class 2P No. 431 works a weekend special train of non-corridor stock over the Lickey Incline circa 1920. The reporting number 89 is not recorded, as this would be a special notice number not listed in the working timetable.

W. Leslie Good, P. B. Whitehouse Collection

Plate 108: Johnson 'spinner' No. 683, carrying a No. 3 Shed Plate, drops down the bank just south of Blackwell Station around 1920. Note the two signals behind the train, and the brakemen's huts adjacent to them. All 'down' freight trains had to stop for pinning down brakes.

W. Leslie Good, P. B. Whitehouse Collection

Plate 109: A Johnson Class 2F 0-6-0, No. 3104, makes her way slowly up the bank at the head of a pick-up freight, circa 1920. There are two engines on the rear, one of which appears to be 'Big Bertha' which is not surprising, with a load of 33 wagons. Note the backplate fitted to the tender, and the springs above its running plate. The distant signal is 'off' for Blackwell.

W. Leslie Good, P. B. Whitehouse Collection

Plate 110: Pictured while at work at the bottom of the bank, No. 2290 passes through Bromsgrove Station. Note the incline beginning virtually from the platform end, and that the train contains four LNWR vehicles indicating that it is probably a west to north express.

P. B. Whitehouse Collection

Plate 111: The Banker when new. As Britain's only ten-coupled locomotive at the time and Derby's pride and joy, No. 2290 was specially built to assist trains up the formidable 1 in 37.7 Lickey Incline, north of Bromsgrove. Probably descended in lineage from the heavy 2-8-0 built for the Somerset & Dorset Joint Railway, this 1919-built monster came to be nicknamed 'Big Bertha' or 'Big Emma', and was the largest engine to be built by the Midland Railway. She must have looked magnificent in red, and just like a fiery dragon at night. The Shed Plate No. 4 indicates that Bromsgrove was a sub-shed of Worcester, and also of note is that there is no headlamp, this was not fitted until December 1920.

W. Leslie Good, P. B. Whitehouse Collection

The Harborne Railway

Branching off the LNWR Stour Valley line and running 2 miles 39 chains to the pleasant and prosperous village of Harborne, the Harborne Railway was a separate company, operated by the LNWR until Grouping when it was incorporated into the LMS. Opened on 10th August 1874 it was worked from the beginning by Webb tender and tank engines, some of which lasted until the days of nationalisation. The service was frequent and popular, with over twenty trains per day each way, until the Corporation motor bus service began to make inroads, but this was out of the pre-grouping period and well into LMS days. Another reason why it was so successful was that there was no tram service to Harborne, prior to the introduction of the buses. It was originally envisaged (under the Act) that the line would continue to the village of Lapal, on the Midland/GWR joint line from Halesowen Junction to Halesowen, but this was never built. Even at the height of its use, the line had problems with the bottleneck double track into New Street beyond Harborne Junction, meaning that if a main line train was delayed, then so was the Harborne Express. It was not unknown for irate passengers to jump from the train held at Icknield Port Road Station, and catch the nearest tram into the city.

The line had two types of freight traffic. The first was coal to the wharves at Hagley Road and Harborne, while the second was a considerable number of wagons per day to the private sidings of Mitchells & Butlers, one of Birmingham's largest brewers.

Right: A page from a local time table book showing the frequency of trains on the Harborne branch in December 1897. Note that the time table also shows the LNWR Perry Barr circle trains—New Street to New Street.

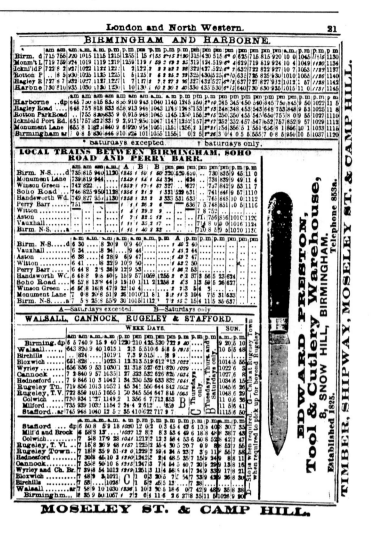

London and North Western. 21
BIRMINGHAM AND HARBORNE.
LOCAL TRAINS BETWEEN BIRMINGHAM, SOHO ROAD AND PERRY BARR.
WALSALL, CANNOCK, RUGELEY & STAFFORD.

EDWARD PRESTON, Tool & Cutlery Warehouse, 8, SNOW HILL, BIRMINGHAM. Established 1825. Telephone 853a.

TIMBER, SHIPWAY, MOSELEY ST. & CAMP HILL.

MOSELEY ST. & CAMP HILL.

Plate 112: Harborne Station circa 1908, with a train entering behind a small LNWR Webb 2-4-2 tank. The signal box shown was shortly to be replaced by one of standard LNWR pattern; there were only two signals, a home and starter.

P. B. Whitehouse Collection

Plate 113: **Harborne Station circa 1912, with an LNWR Webb 18 in. goods 0-6-0 leaving with a New Street-bound train.** In the background is the tower of Harborne Fire Station and, behind the train, carriage sidings which were later used to service the Chad Valley Toy Factory, which made the official GWR jigsaw puzzles.

P. B. Whitehouse Collection

Plate 114: **A train of four-wheeled stock, behind an LNWR Webb 5 ft. 6 in. 2-4-2 tank, climbs the 1 in 66 incline up towards Hagley Road Station.** The picture was taken from the garden of the author's paternal grandfather around 1909.

The Late Mrs A. Whitehouse
P. B. Whitehouse Collection

Lines to the Black Country

Plate 115 (below): The LNWR/GWR joint station at Dudley, circa 1899. The train at the right-hand platform face is hauled by a 2-2-2 locomotive from Wolverhampton which will continue over the Oxford, Worcester & Wolverhampton line. The tracks on the right accommodate the LNWR line from Dudley Port, and the South Staffs line to Walsall.

Dudley Reference Library

Plate 116 (below): One of the 1905 series of LNWR official postcards, showing a train on the Stour Valley line near Smethwick, hauled by a Webb 'Precedent' class 2-4-0 locomotive. The card shows other interesting features of the period including the competition of the canal system, the excellence of the LNWR track, and the company's use of extremely tall signals with repeater arms where obstructions such as bridges were involved. The bridge in the foreground is Galton Bridge, built by Thomas Telford whilst that in the background carries the GWR line from Handsworth Junction to Stourbridge and Worcester.

P. B. Whitehouse Collection

TRAIN NEAR SMETHWICK. STOUR VALLEY LINE.

Plate 117 (above): **A turn of the century photograph of a Halesowen to Old Hill branch train climbing up towards Haden Hill Tunnel. The engine is probably a 517 class 0-4-2 tank, and the train behind is comprised of oil-lighted four wheelers.**

Sandwell Public Library

Plate 118: This is a photograph of a remarkable engine, most of whose sisters had gone by 1907. Taken at Wolverhampton circa 1911/12—No. 110 was withdrawn there in May 1912. It was the last of Joseph Armstrong's '111 Class' to be built, and was almost certainly reconstructed out of two early Wolverhampton singles along with its sister engine, No. 30. This work was carried out on No. 110 in 1887, and on No. 30 in 1886, with the original locomotives dating from 1863. They were probably the first GWR standard gauge engines to be fitted with copper capped chimneys, and No. 110 is one of the engines mentioned by Ahrons as working over the Wolverhampton to Chester line in the latter part of the 19th century.

H. W. Burman, P. B. Whitehouse Collection

Plate 119: Oxley sidings at Wolverhampton, photographed in 1900. Note the tall wooden post and arm signal, the six-wheeled oil lit coaches, and the double-framed 0-6-0 at the head of a short goods train.

Central Library, Wolverhampton

Plate 120: the frontage of the GWR's Low Level station, Wolverhampton, in 1908. This well-posed photograph shows Hansom cabs, a horse-drawn parcels van and various dignitaries standing about in bowler hats. Note the GWR buses in the background.

Central Library, Wolverhampton

Plates 121–123 (above, below, and right upper): **Three** views of the LNWR's High Level station at Wolverhampton, with tw
exterior photographs taken in 1908 and one of the interior taken in 1910. Note the Midland Railway board to the centre of th
picture, and the GWR's (for access to Low Level) to the left. The destinations listed are countrywide, with the Midlan
being as diverse as Walsall, Manchester, Liverpool, Sheffield, Leeds, Bradford and Bristol, whilst the LNWR offered trains
Birmingham, Leamington, London, Gloucester, Swansea, Bristol, Bournemouth, Plymouth, Burton, Derby, Leicest
Dublin and Belfast, amongst others.

Central Library, Wolverhampt

ate 124: The LNWR goods yard at Wolverhampton in
)8. Note the furniture containers to the left of the
otograph.

Central Library, Wolverhampton

Plate 125: The Midland Railway goods yard at Wolverhampton, circa 1908.
Central Library, Wolverhampton

Plate 126: LNWR Webb 4 ft. 6 in. 2-4-2 ta[nk]
No. 908, built in September 1890, phot[o-]
graphed at Walsall Station circa 1908.
Walsall Public Libra[ry]

Plate 127 (right top): The GWR's Ox[ley]
Shed, probably circa 1910. Note the 'Bulld[og]'
and 'City' class 4-4-0s on the left, the t[wo]
turntables, and the older 0-6-0s on the rig[ht.]
The shed foreman in his bowler stands to t[he]
left of the pit on the through road.
Central Library, Wolverhampt[on]

Plate 128 (right bottom): Walsall Stati[on]
frontage, probably just prior to the Grou[p-]
ing, as there are signs that part of it is bei[ng]
demolished to make way for the 1923 buil[d-]
ing.

Walsall Public Libra[ry]

Birmingham (Snow Hill) Station)

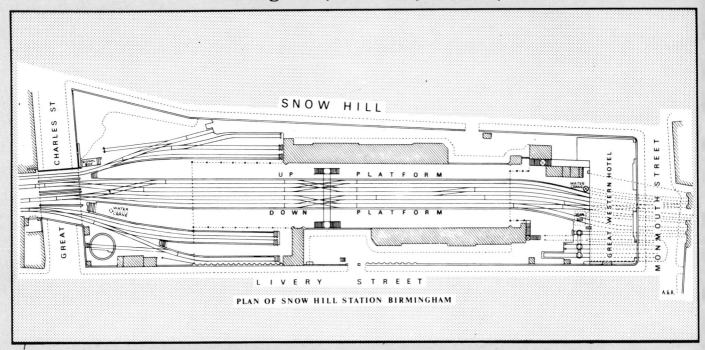

Plan of the trackwork and station layout of Snow Hill Station after the first reconstruction in 1871.

D. A. C. Harrison Collection

Plan of the trackwork, signals and station layout of Snow Hill Station after the second reconstruction 1906–1912. The track layout is shown in its original form with the double scissors crossovers.

British Rail

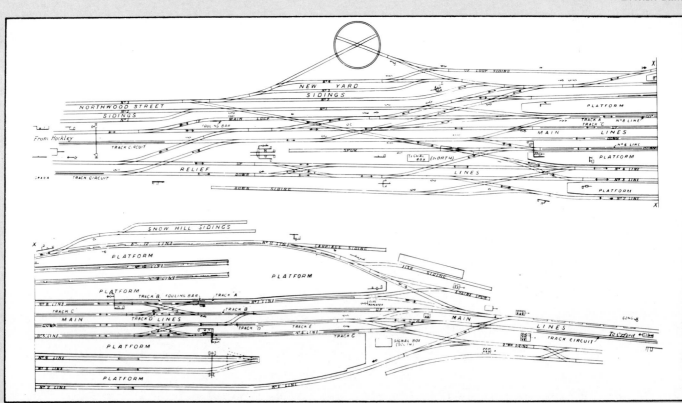

Plate 129 (right): The Livery Street entrance to Snow Hill Station, probably photographed in the 1890s. Note the typical city cobbled street of the period. Examination of the print shows that the buildings are somewhat different to those shown on Edwardian photographs, and with the absence of traffic in the yard, the above date is a suggested one.

The late George Whitehouse, Courtesy Birmingham Reference Library

Great Charles Street or Livery Street were the names given to Birmingham's first GWR station, which was opened to broad gauge trains from Paddington in October 1852. The special to mark the through working was appropriately hauled by Daniel Gooch's *Lord of the Isles* which, sadly, ran into the back of a mixed train at Aynho although fortunately, only minor injuries occurred.

The lines into Birmingham from the south-east were mixed gauge, as any through services to the north had to use standard gauge tracks. Full conversion to standard gauge took place in 1869.

The station remained a terminus until 14th November 1854, when the new line from Wolverhampton came into operation. The GWR had hoped to be able to use the old Shrewsbury & Birmingham powers to run over the Stour Valley to Navigation Street (later New Street), but this was prevented by an astute LNWR and its lawyers.

The name Snow Hill came into existence in February 1858, the first station was a temporary wooden structure rebuilt in 1871. Shortly after the second station was constructed, the familiar south side tunnel was extended and completed, with the tracks running through a blue brick retaining walled-cutting until 1874. Later, it was a cut and cover process, and a pedestrian way, still known as the Great Western Arcade, was built on top of it, with an entrance right opposite the reconstructed Great Western Railway Hotel, which was first built in 1863. The old wooden station was re-erected at Didcot.

The following thirty years showed little change, but increased traffic led to considerable track improvements, and these were put in hand from September 1906 when a start on remodelling the station began, with the work being completed early in 1914. One of the factors leading to reorganisation was the proposal to construct the Ashendon & Aynho railway. This work began in December 1906 and was finished in April 1910. The new station was designed by Walter Armstrong, Works Engineer for the GWR. There were two main problems, the first being that lateral expansion was impossible because of existing thoroughfares and secondly, on the south side, there was a permanent bottle-neck in the form of the 596 yd long tunnel, the widening of which would have been quite impractical.

The new station was built with two large island platforms having two through centre tracks and bays at the north end of each platform. Because of the lateral problems the platforms were lengthy, provision being made for two trains to be accommodated on the main up and down faces.

Lengths were as follows:

'Down' relief platforms Nos. 1 and 2	1,180 ft.
'Down' main platforms Nos. 5 and 6	1,188 ft.
'Up' main platforms Nos. 7 and 8	1,197 ft.
'Up' relief platforms Nos. 11 and 12	971 ft.

(Latterly, these numbers were reversed)

Unlike New Street, Snow Hill was a closed station, access being via a forward circulating area bounded by Snow Hill, Colmore Row and Livery Street, two broad covered walkways and steps down to the platforms.

With the new track improvements, there were four tracks coming in from Handsworth Junction in the north, and widening took place from the south from the end of the tunnel. Moor Street Station opened for the new North Warwick line traffic on 1st July 1909.

Openings of the widened sections were as follows:

Olton to Tyseley	January 1907
Tyseley to Small Heath (South)	May 1908
Small Heath (South) to Small Heath (North)	July 1910
Bordesley to Moor Street Station	16th November 1913
Small Heath to Bordesley	1914

By 1909, the GWR had also reorganised the signalling, introducing to Snow Hill the Siemens all-electrical system with the whole station controlled from two boxes, the north containing 244 levers and the south 80. The number of signals was considerably reduced, by the use of Annett type installations with route indicators.

Full and detailed information is contained in the August 1911 issue of the *Great Western Railway Magazine* and the 2nd June 1911 issue of *Engineering*.

Plate 130: Snow Hill Station, shortly before demolition in 1907/8. The overall roof is a shabby affair compared with the fifty year old New Street, and the railway a poor relation as far as London traffic was concerned. On the left is the roof over the old booking hall area and in the yard, adjacent to Livery Street, are a few Hansom cabs and horse-drawn railway vans. In the 'up' platform, a 39XX class 2-6-2 tank, one of a class which was rebuilt by Churchward in 1907–10 from Dean goods 0-6-0 locomotives (most of which worked in the Birmingham area), heads a close-coupled suburban set of six wheelers. Almost certainly, the view was taken from the Great Western Hotel in Colmore Row.

British Railways, D. A. C. Harrison Collection

Plate 131: A scene at Snow Hill during the reconstruction of the station, taken from inside the new south tunnel. In the foreground is one of the 2-4 suburban tanks, whilst above are the girders forming the base for the new booking offices and circulating areas.

City of Birmingham Public Librari

Plate 132: 'Queen' class 2-2-2 No. 999 *Sir Alexander*, at Snow Hill in 1898. Built in 1875, it was one of ten of the class to carry names. For many years, these engines worked the London to Wolverhampton expresses, and this continued until about 1900 when a larger turntable was installed at Stafford Road Shed to take the bigger 4-4-2s and 4-4-0s. By 1904, the class had become obsolescent and No. 999 was one of the early withdrawals. No. 1128 was the last locomotive to go, being withdrawn as late as April 1914.

Warwick County Record Office

Plate 133: Curved framed 'Bulldog' class No. 3340 *Marazion*, with combined number and nameplate on the cabside, is seen at Snow Hill in 1901.

Warwick County Record Office

Plate 134: A scene in the new circulating area, which was to remain almost unchanged until the station's demolition. Of particular interest is the vast and ornate poster-board, with the inscription 'GWR The Holiday Line' in gold at the top. The poster advertising trains to London(expensive, at 8s 9d and 5s 6d in 1911) points out that this is the shortest route and is flanked by 'up' and 'down' departure bills with local time-tables beneath. Overhead, the signboard proudly declares the availability of the new (1908) route to the south - west, via Stratford-on-Avon, Cheltenham and Gloucester. The two magnificent cars on the right are reputed to be a Wolseley and a 20 hp Renault of about 1904/8, the Renault's registration of 0-80 being an early Birmingham one.

British Railways, D. A. C. Harrison Collection

Plate 135: The 'down' platforms at Snow Hill in 1911, showing the two bays looking towards Hockley in the rebuilt station. Construction work is not entirely complete, as can be seen by the cast-iron columns for the lift lying on the platform, the temporary wooden fencing and scaffolding, plus that dangerous looking ladder on the left.

British Railways, D. A. C. Harrison Collection

Plate 136: The main 'up' platform in 1911, looking north towards Hockley. The gates for the lift are now in place, and the two bay platforms are available for trains. Note the 'print your name' machine to the right of the photograph, which was something which remained, still at one penny, until the station's closure to main line traffic in 1967.

British Railways, D. A. C. Harrison Collection

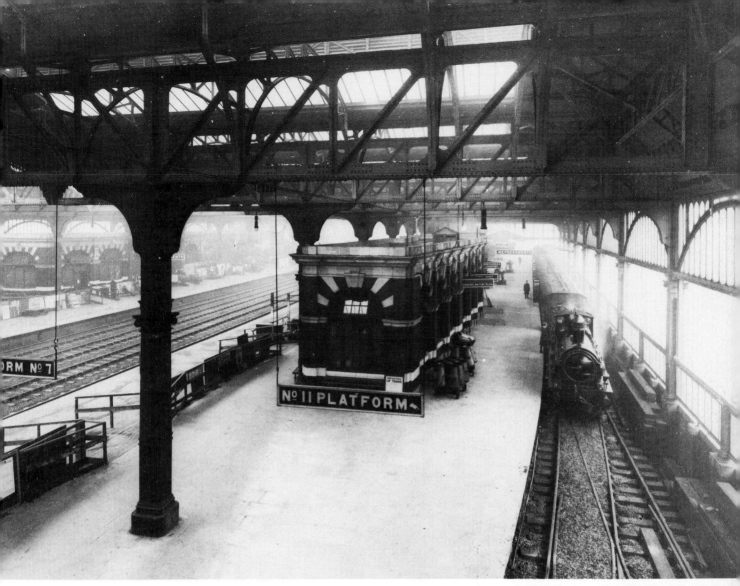

te 137 (above): The new Snow Hill Station of 1912, with
ch interior faces of the island platforms barricaded from the
in platform areas for reasons which cannot be explained at
time of writing. The locomotive, heading an 'up' express at
tform 11, later renumbered to platform 12, is an outside-
med 2-4-0, and true to the 'boys of all ages' GWR tradition,
oung man is inspecting the footplate. All the tracks have
n recently ballasted, and indeed close inspection of the
nt-hand side of the picture shows the brand-new rail and
epers, expected in this just completed station. The billboard,
n above the sign for platform 11, lists the departure times of
' trains whilst that on the left of the photograph covers the
etable for the Birmingham area.

British Railways

te 138: The sector table at the south end of the 'down' bay
tforms, in the form of a moveable point; note the operating
ndles in the left foreground. This photograph, showing a
nverted Dean 0-6-0 as 2-6-2 tank No. 3907 with a copper-
pped chimney, was taken in 1910. The station staff are
viously very interested in the proceedings, everything has
en nicely posed; apart from normal uniformed staff, the
tion master is in evidence in his top hat (centre of third
ach from right), and there are at least three bowler-hatted
pectors.

British Railways, D. A. C. Harrison Collection

Plate 139: The exterior of Snow Hill Station, taken from Colmore Row circa 1908/10, showing clearly the dining rooms and refreshment areas. The sign over the archway reads 'PASSENGER ENTRANCE'. Note the Public Works Department with the 'no thoroughfare' boards across the tracks and the cobblestones between them.

British Railways

Plate 140: One of the combined number and nameplate 'Atbara' class 4-4-0 locomotives, No. 3383 *Omdurman* (later No. 4130), as station pilot around 1912. The 'Atbara' class dated from 1900 (hence their names—which were associated with the Boer War), and were first used in the West Midlands on the Paddington to Wolverhampton main line, which had only just been opened to engines of this size. Later, around the date of this photograph, they worked the Birmingham to Swansea trains as well as short distance semi-fasts in Birmingham, Leamington, Banbury and Oxford areas.

H. W. Burman, P. B. Whitehouse Collection

Plate 141: One of Swindon's 2-4-2 tanks of the turn of the century, No. 3616, shown carrying a local train headlamp below the chimney. The date is unknown, but a clue is given by the chocolate and cream coach/van behind the bunker. Most of H. W. Burman's photographs of Snow Hill were 1911/3, when coaches would have been newly-painted in the lake livery. Note the clearly marked lining out on the bunker sides, and the padlock on the toolbox on the running plate—tools were as easily 'borrowed' then as now. The engines were designed for fast suburban work, especially in the Birmingham area.

H. W. Burman, P. B. Whitehouse Collection

Plate 142: Churchward's 4-4-0 'County' class, No. 3479 *County of Warwick* (later No. 3836), photographed at Snow Hill on 3rd July 1911, while still a saturated locomotive. These engines worked the new Birmingham to Bristol expresses over the North Warwick line via Stratford-on-Avon and Cheltenham. Observe the gas cylinder wagon to the left of the tender, and the coach on the right painted in the new GWR lake livery.

H. W. Burman, P. B. Whitehouse Collection

The Great Western South-East of Birmingham

Until the turn of the century, the lines from Snow Hill to the south were a shadow of those which evolved during the Edwardian era, with trains running the 'Great Way Round' to London via Oxford and Didcot, plus local services to Solihull, or well into the countryside at Knowle.

The year 1899 saw the independent Birmingham, North Warwickshire & Stratford-upon-Avon Railway coming to terms with the GWR; making junctions with it at Tyseley and Bearley and abandoning its independent entry into Birmingham. Meanwhile, the extension of the Stratford to Honeybourne branch to make a through main line to Cheltenham opened up a completely new scene, there was

now an extra route in the offing from Birmingham to the south-west. This, together with general modernisation in the form of track re-laying, station rebuilding and the entry of Churchward on to the locomotive front—and coupled with the later (July 1910) cut-off line to London—made all the difference to the West Midlands situation. Snow Hill was rebuilt, the tracks were widened, and suburban services revamped.

The following photographs show the changes which appeared in trains and motive power between the old era and the new.

Plate 143: Solihull Station at the turn of the century, looking towards Birmingham. At that period and before the later widening, there was a small coal yard adjacent to the 'up' platform. The notice, with its typical GWR cast-iron letters pinned to a wooden board, prohibits passengers from crossing the track except by the footbridge.

Solihull Public Library

Plate 144: An 'up' local train, behind a 2-2-2 locomotive (possibly No. 999 *Sir Alexander*), approaches Solihull in 1898. Note the siding with the old baulk track, which is a relic of the mixed gauge days.

Warwick County Record Office

Plate 145: A Great Western Railway guard awaits the 'right away' with the 9.15 a.m. local service from Solihull to Birmingham (Snow Hill) in 1899. Note the outside communication cord on the coach, which appears to be very slack.

Warwick County Record Office

Plate 146: The final batch of broad gauge ta[n]k engines for the GWR (Nos. 3541–3559) w[ere] designed by William Dean in 1888/9 for work[ing] in Devon and Cornwall. This was virtually [the] end for the 7 ft. 0 in. gauge, so they were nat[ur]ally constructed as convertibles, being a mod[ifi]cation of the existing 35XX class of stand[ard] gauge side tanks. Although originally desig[ned] as 0-4-2 saddle tanks, these proved so unstea[dy] that they were all altered to 0-4-4 short side a[nd] back tank engines. The class was converted [to] standard gauge in 1892. Even though the 0-[4-4] tank was an improvement, these engines s[uf]fered from unsteadiness at the trailing end, a[nd] were rebuilt as 4-4-0 tender engines betwe[en] 1899 and 1902. In 1898, an unknown member [of] the class was in the Birmingham Division, and [is] seen here with a Snow Hill to Stratford lo[cal] train.

Warwick County Record Off[ice]

Plate 147: One of the long-lived **GWR** 517 class 0-4-2Ts, No. 215 at Solihull in 1900. This veteran, built in 1876, lasted in service until 1934; it was fitted with auto-train apparatus for the last two decades of its life. These 0-4-2T locomotives bore the brunt of the branch line and local work in the Northern Division, especially in the Birmingham and Wolverhampton areas.

Warwick County Record Office

Plate 148: One of the 1902 batch of 3600 class GWR 2-4-2 tanks, built with bunker coal rails and photographed as new at Solihull sometime that year. Note the lining round the tank sides, and the smart shunter on the footplate steps.

Warwick County Record Office

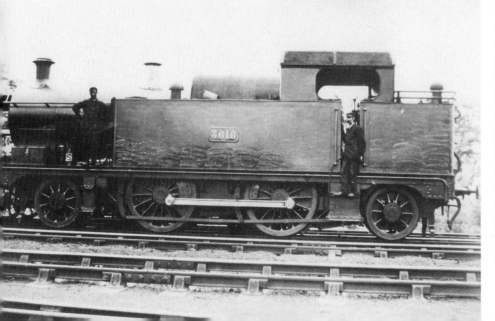

The main line between Widney Manor and Knowle, sometime between 1911 and 1913. This was a particularly interesting period, as a large number of improvements had taken place in the previous five years, including the opening of the North Warwick line, the rebuilding of Snow Hill Station, and the general widening from Handsworth Junction to Olton. New classes were also beginning to appear in earnest, with Churchward having replaced Dean, 4-6-0s ousting 2-4-0s, and 4-4-0s on the expresses even though singles continued to appear with some regularity. The variety of motive power is clearly shown in the following reproductions.

Eight different GWR classes heading 'up' trains while approaching Bentley Heath Crossing between 1910 and 1913. This was one of H. W. Burman's favourite photographic locations, as there were clear views of trains in each direction.

Plate 149: 3232 class 2-4-0, No. 3237 of October 1892, sports express headlamps. Notice that the second, third and fourth coaches carry head-boards, so the train is of some importance. These locomotives were the last completely new 2-4-0s to be built at Swindon, and the numbers on the cabsides were mounted separately on a curve, not enclosed on a plate as normal practice. No. 3237 was a Wolverhampton (Stafford Road) engine for many years, ending her life there in 1928.
H. W. Burman, P. B. Whitehouse Collection

Plate 150: Curved-framed 'Badminton' class 4-4-0 No. 3298 (later 4106) Grosvenor, of June 1898, is seen with the 12.07 p.m. ex-Snow Hill to Paddington train on 26th June 1911. The train is of the modern stock, except for one solitary clerestory in the middle.
H. W. Burman, P. B. Whitehouse Collection

Plate 151: A Standard Goods 0-6-0 (possibly No. 397) heads an 'up' goods between Widney Manor and Bentley Heath on 28th September 1910.
H. W. Burman, P. B. Whitehouse Collection

Plate 152: Straight-framed 'Badmin[ton' class 4-4-0 *Earl Cawdor,* car[ry]ing its new number 4105, heads [the] 11.15 a.m. ex-Snow Hill train on 2[?] September 1910. For a ti[me] (1903–1906), the engine had a la[rge] flush round-topped boiler on tr[ial] and also incorporated an equa[lly] large side-windowed cab reminisce[nt] of North Eastern Railway cabs.
*H. W. Burman, P. B. Whitehou[se Collecti[on]

Plate 153: One of the 'Armstrong', 388 or Standard Goods 0-6-0 loco-motives, No. 397 of December 1866, as it nears Bentley Heath Crossing with a fast goods train circa 1910. Note the three lamps on the buffer beam, which was the old headcode for a mineral train. No. 397 was one of the old Northern Division engines permanently attached to the Wolver-hampton area; it was withdrawn in December 1919.
H. W. Burman, P. B. Whitehouse Collection

Plate 154: Suburban 2-4-2 tank N[o.] 3604, with the 11.20 a.m. all statio[ns] Snow Hill to Leamington train, o[n] 24th September 1910. Note the clos[e] coupled suburban stock all in t[he] new lake livery, bar the last vehic[le] which is still in chocolate and crea[m.] *H. W. Burman, P. B. Whitehou[se Collecti[on]

Plate 155: An 'up' Oxford and London express behind 'County' class 4-[4]-0 No. 3814 *County of Chester,* which was *County of Cheshire* until [M]ay 1907. it is seen on 26th June [19]11, with the 12.07 p.m. Snow Hill [to] Paddington via Oxford and Reading train.
[H.] *W. Burman, P. B. Whitehouse Collection*

Plate 156: 'Saint' class 4-6-0 No. 2911 *Saint Agatha* of August 1907, passing Bentley Heath with the 2.50 p.m. fast train to Paddington.
H. W. Burman, P. B. Whitehouse Collection

Plate 157: No. 4023 *King George* of June 1909, is seen with the 2.45 p.m. ex-Snow Hill train on 19th April 1912. With the coming of the 'King' class, this engine was renamed *The Danish Monarch* on July 1927. It was renamed again in October 1927 becoming *Danish Monarch* and ran unnamed from November 1940 until withdrawal in July 1952.
H. W. Burman, P. B. Whitehouse Collection

'Down' trains of the same period [ar]e reflected by six classes, ranging [fr]om Singles to Stars. These pictures [po]rtray the short two loop four track [se]ction between Knowle & Dorridge [st]ation and Bentley Heath Crossing, [a] situation that remained until the [wi]dening of 1933 when the four [tr]acks ran through from Olton to [K]nowle.

Plate 158: Dean Single No. 30[] *Great Britain,* of March 1892, tak[] the 3.28 p.m. 'down' local servi[] from Knowle & Dorridge towar[] Bentley Heath on 9th April 19[]. The engine was originally built as [] final development of the 2-2-2, b[] was rebuilt in November 1894. Al[] known as the 'Achilles' class, t[] conversion became vital after a de[] ailment in Box Tunnel on 16[] December 1892. Further rebuildi[] of some members of the cla[] (including No. 3013) took pla[] between 1905/6, and later in 1909.[] 1910 No. 3013, along with most [] her sisters, received the new sma[] Belpaire boiler as shown in the ph[] tograph.
H. W. Burman, P. B. Whitehou[]
Collecti[]

Plate 159: Another 'Achilles' class 4-2-2, but with name and number unknown (but possibly 3027 *Worcester* which was based in the West Midlands), double-heads an outside-framed 0-6-0 with a 'down' fast train circa 1910. The engine is shown in its 1900 rebuilt condition with a No. 2 standard boiler and cast-iron chimney. The 0-6-0, coupled as pilot behind the train engine was normal GWR practice, and was no doubt attached at Leamington, the train being too heavy for a single wheeler to take unaided up Hatton Bank.
H. W. Burman, P. B. Whitehouse
Collection

Plate 160: One of the 7 ft. 0 in. non[] inal rebuilds of 1894, No. 7 (ne[] number 4171) *Armstrong,* which w[] originally named *Charles Saunder[]*. There were only four in the clas[] which theoretically replaced four [] 4-0 locomotives. No. 7 was always [] standard gauge engine, but the oth[] three, Nos. 8, 14 and 16, were broa[] gauge convertibles. The date of th[] photograph is unknown, but th[] whole class was sent to the Wolve[] hampton Division between 1909 an[] 1911.
H. W. Burman P. B. Whitehouse Co[]
lectio[]

te 161: 'County' class 4-4-0 No.
4 County of Chester leaves
owle & Dorridge with the 12.30
vice from Paddington to Birm-
ham and Wolverhampton, via
ord, on 25th August 1913.
*W. Burman, P. B. Whitehouse
Collection*

Plate 162: An early 'Saint' class 4-6-
0, No. 2901 *Lady Superior,* which
was built in May 1906 but not named
until October. This was the first locomotive with a modern Schmidt
superheated boiler to be built and
run on a British Railway. The date of
the photograph is August 1913 and
possibly, the engine was running in
after a repair, as goods turn would
be very unusual for a 'Saint' at this
time.
*H. W. Burman, P. B. Whitehouse
Collection*

te 163: An unknown 'Star' class
-0, with what appears to be the
yal Train between Knowle &
rridge and Bentley Heath Cross-
, circa 1910–3. There is no record
this photograph in the Burman
s in the author's possession, but in
w of the normal class A head-
ps, this was certainly not the full
yal Train. Quite possibly, it was
er an e.c.s. working, or was con-
ing members of the Royal Family
er than the King or Queen.
*W. Burman, P. B. Whitehouse
Collection*

Plates 164 & 165: The 3.28
'down' local service to Snow
leaves Widney Manor behind
different classes during April 1
The assumption of the date is n
on the basis of the tree to the
being leafless, with the actual dat
the photograph of No. 3050 b
given by H. W. Burman as 1st A
1913, while the 4-4-0 has only 1
as the date. Note the similar set
stock, bar the addition of the
wheeled milk van behind No. 3
Also note the vacuum reservoir
the roof of each of the clerest
coaches—almost certainly slip
hicles either empty stock or pic
up at Leamington. The locomot
concerned are 'Achilles' class
8 in. Single No. 3050 *Royal Sovere*
of February 1895, and an unkno
41XX class 4-4-0. There is a prob
area in the date, as No. 3050
reported to have been fitted with
small Belpaire boiler in 1914,
stated in part seven of *The Lo
motives of the Great Western R
way,* published by the RCTS F
G9.

*H. W. Burman, P. B. Whiteho
Collect*

The following photographs sh
four local trains and an express
Knowle & Dorridge, between 19
and 1918. All are 'up' trains.

Plate 166: The very last of
'Queen' class 2-2-2s to remain
service, No. 1128 of June 1875, w
withdrawn in April 1914. The lo
motive is seen here on one of
latter day passenger turns on
unspecified date, but likely to
around 1910–12. It was an Oxfo
engine, and it is recorded in t
RCTS's *Locomotives of the Gre
Western Railway* as having been se
with a cross-country express betwe
Oxford and Banbury a few wee
before its withdrawal.

*H. W. Burman, P. B. Whitehou
Collecti*

ate 167: A 'Barnum' or 3206 class -0, No. 3212, stands at Knowle & rridge Station with an 'up' local n on an unknown date, but pro-ly between 1911 and 1913. A nber of the class were stationed at ford during that period, and the n is likely to be a semi-fast service m Snow Hill.

W. Burman, P. B. Whitehouse
Collection

ate 168: A 2301 or 'Dean goods' ss 0-6-0, No. 2579 is seen at owle & Dorridge with an 'up' al train on an unknown date but ly to be between 1910 and 1913. te the engine is still carrying its per-capped chimney.

W. Burman, P. B. Whitehouse
Collection

ate 169: No. 3823 *County of Car-von* is about to leave Knowle & rridge with the 10.20 a.m. 'up' ex-ss from Snow Hill on 18th April 2.

W. Burman, P. B. Whitehouse
Collection

Plate 170: Hatton Stati▮
between 1905 and 1910, with ▮
London-bound train entering ▮
hind a double-framed 4-4-0. N▮
the station nameboard at t▮
north end of the 'down' platfo▮
telling passengers to change ▮
Stratford-on-Avon, and the c▮
wagons sitting in the siding ▮
hind the 'up' platform palings.
Shakespeare Birthplace Tr▮

Plate 171: Hatton Station sometime between 1910 and 1914 (dated by the Belpaire firebox and boiler on the 'Achilles' class 4-2-2 standing in the Stratford-on-Avon branch platform). The photograph shows the scene looking south and is taken from the roadbridge. The locomotiveless train on the 'down' main line is unusual and it is possible that the 4-2-2 is picking up coaches from the branch to transfer to a Birmingham bound train.

Warwick County Museum

Stratford-on-Avon

Two photographs of the station at Stratford-on-Avon, taken around 1909/10, looking towards Leamington or Birmingham. The make-up of the train is particularly interesting, as it comprises a Dean saddle tank, 4 four-wheeled oil lamped non-corridor coaches, a van and what appears to be a destination-boarded corridor vehicle at the rear. This indicates a train from Leamington with a through coach from London which could well be the old 11.25 a.m. ex-Paddington train, slipping at Leamington at 1.18 p.m., leaving at 1.30 p.m. and arriving at Stratford at 2.00 p.m. This would accord with the shadows. Note the wheel tapper/examiner, with his hammer adjacent to the footplate. The poster-board, lying close to the wooden trestle, is headed London & North Western Railway while the nameboard on the left-hand platform reads Platform for Bearley Junction and Leamington, indicating that the North Warwick line is open. Advertisements include Lanola (makes the skin soft as velvet), Hotel Cecil, Lipton's Tea (largest sales in the world), Maple & Co. London & Paris (first class furniture), Van Houten's Cocoa (best & goes farthest) and Pears Soap.

Plates 172 & 173 (below and overleaf): The platform level photograph shows not only the station's plain clothes staff on parade, but also two clear 1891 dates, both adjacent to the GWR monograms that decorate the cast-iron footbridge. Advertisements include Bovril, Mitchells & Butlers (Cape Hill Brewery Birmingham), Stones Ginger Wine, Petter Oil Engines, *Daily Sketch,* Bobby & Co. Leamington Spa (latest fashions), as well as the ubiquitous Stephens' Inks. The map shows details of the GWR system, and its connection to Ireland.

Shakespeare Birthplace Trust

Branch Line

Plate 174: A reproduction o
postcard of Great Alne Stati
on the Alcester branch, ci
1906.

Shakespeare Birthplace Tr

Great Alne Station.

The LNWR in Coventry and Leamington

These drawings were reproduced in the *Illustrated London News* of 14th December 1844, along with the following text:
OPENING OF THE LEAMINGTON AND WARWICK RAILWAY

The 'opening train', unadorned, and in simple business guise—according to the custom of the London and Birmingham Company, who seem to have a natural horror of flags and bands of music—left Coventry a little after nine o'clock in the morning; and although the weather was far from propitious, its departure was witnessed and cheered by a vast multitude of well-dressed spectators. In its course past the numerous bridges, which give a character to the rail, and at other good points of observation, the same testimonies of respect were paid to the 'courageous' inmates of the snug 'first classes' on this, their gallant venture. At Kenilworth, many ladies graced the triumph with their presence, and some danger was incurred by their very close proximity to the rails. At Leamington an immense assemblage of respectable persons, together with the elite of the neighbourhood, received the train, which was hereafter to put them within three hours and a half of the metropolis, with every mark of intelligent gratulation. The day then became a universal holiday. Business was everywhere suspended, festivities of 'all sorts' were interchanged by the delighted people, and, at night a grand dinner given to the directors and friends of the railway, came off in grand style at the Regent's Hotel, and crowned the 'opening day'. To those who would wish for particulars, we may say that the dinner was served at six o'clock, and that upwards of fifty first-rate gentlemen sat down to it. Capt. Musgrave (in place of Dr. Jephson) took the chair, supported by the Hon. and Rev. Mr. Somerville, Mr. Wilkinson,, Mr. Stracey, Mr. Drinkwater, and other gentlemen connected with the county. The dinner, consisting of all the delicacies of the season, was served with their usual skill and precision by Messrs. Breach and Jeffereys. A deputation from the Nuneaton and Bedworth Railway Company, headed by Mr. Wilkinson, chairman, was present, and added greatly to the good fellowship of the meeting.

The tract of country through which the railway passes is picturesque in the extreme; well wooded hills, luxuriant meadows, and fertile valleys, alternate with romantic villages, and sites of abiding historic interest. The remains of Stoneleigh Abbey, Kenilworth Castle and Abbey, Warwick Castle in the immediate neighbourhood, may be cited in illustration.

The distinguishing feature of the line (which for the present consists only of a single pair of rails) is found in the undulatory character of its gradients. The entire length rises and falls like the surface of a gently rolling ocean taken at any one moment of time, and these 'ups and downs', or dips, as they are called, are so contrived that the impetus acquired in running down one incline is contrived exactly to compensate for the retardation of the succeeding ascent. An obvious example of this mode of construction occurs in the Melbourne valley, as shown in the accompanying engraving. The valley is of considerable depth, and in the formation of a permanent way across it, it was held expedient to build, not a horizontal, but a curved viaduct, the lowest point being near the centre, a mode of procedure which has produced a great saving of material, and a considerable gain in the working speed. It is built of brick and stone and consists of seventeen elliptical arches, each thirty feet span.

The stations are remarkable for convenience of arrangement, and simplicity of design. the one at Kenilworth is an elegant and very light structure, fitted with spacious booking-offices, comfortable waiting-rooms, &c.; and stands within a quarter of a mile of the village, with excellent approaches, and covered reception arcade, for carriages and passengers. We give a view of it, as a model of its kind.

The Leamington Terminus, about midway between, and immediately adjoining the turnpike road from Warwick to Leamington, near the Birmingham and Warwick Canal, contains all necessary accommodation for the usual routine of railway business; but, throughout, of a greatly superior character. The waiting-rooms are replete with every modern accommodation, and are elegantly furnished with ottomans, couches, &c. The booking-offices are fitted with care for the prompt dispatch of business. At the north end is an Italian tower, intended for the reception of a forcing-pump and reservoir of water, so that a jet of water, in case of fire, may be instantly obtained.

The stations, and all the works on the line, as well as the formation of the permanent way, have been designed and carried out by Robert B. Dockray, Esq., the resident

NILWORTH STATION.

engineer to the London and Birmingham Railway Company.

The length of the line is nearly nine miles; and the sum expended in its construction amounts to nearly £175,000 a very large sum, the excess having been incurred in the purchase of expensive lands.

MELBOURNE GRANGE VIADUCT.

LEAMINGTON TERMINUS.

Once the LNWR had managed to exclude the GWR from Coventry by constructing the branch from Leamington, Warwick and Kenilworth, it obtained a virtual monopoly of the city's railway traffic, the only other contender being the Midland Railway, which gained running powers from Nuneaton in 1860. Strangely, this was only observed in the running of goods trains from 1865 onwards. Nevertheless the city was well served both by main line expresses and suburban services; as the London fast trains stopped (and continue to stop) there, whilst the link to Birmingham has always been good. In the period under review, the train service through to Leamington was extended until it reached its zenith, although services continued to operate until sometime into natonalisation. Such was the rivalry between the LNWR and the GWR that no real use was made of the link between Coventry and Leamington until the 1970s. In the period covered by this book, students of locomotive power could see most of the principal express classes belonging to each of the two companies in either station, but the links either via Berkswell or Coventry made general use of older classes, which were replaced and put out to grass alongside the ubiquitous Webb tank engines.

Early Days of the London & Birmingham

Plate 175 (left): An 1830s engraving by W. Rádclyffe, with a distant view of Coventry, and a London & Birmingham Railway train near Earlsdon Lane Bridge.

Coventry City Library

Plate 176 (below): A print showing Coventry's first station, circa 1840.

Coventry City Library

Coventry Station

Plate 177: Coventry Station around 1860, looking towards Birmingham and prior to the rebuilding of the 'up' platform. Note the weather protection provided for all trains both 'up' and 'down', the luggage racks on the coach roof to the left, and the three arm slotted signal, complete with ornate finial, on the right. Although the date is given as 1860, this may be a little early considering the gas lamp in the foreground.

Coventry City Library

Plate 178: Coventry Station with 'up' passenger and freight trains, probably around 1879. The passenger train is headed by one of the famous LNWR 'Large Bloomers', which were designed by McConnell for the Southern Division in 1851, whilst the freight engine is a 'DX' Class 0-6-0. The 2-2-2 is No. 851 *Apollo* (Sharp No. 251), as rebuilt by F. W. Webb and which received its name in 1872; it also received a Webb cab in 1878/9. *Apollo* carries the then new LNWR lined out black livery whilst the 'DX', displaying some Webb modifications, is in the old colours. Note that although from the shadows, the photograph appears to have been taken in high summer it is still a time exposure, as shown by the blurring of the water-column bag and the steam from the safety-valves of the 'DX'.

Coventry City Library

Plate 179: Coventry Station, circa 1900, looking towards Birmingham. The train, a local working, headed by either a 'DX' or an 18 in. goods 0-6-0, and containing three carriage trucks, has just passed under the Warwick Road Bridge. The clock on the platform shows that it is 10.12 a.m., which could indicate a late running 9.15 a.m. service from Birmingham (New Street), proceeding on to Rugby at 10.10 a.m.

Coventry City Library

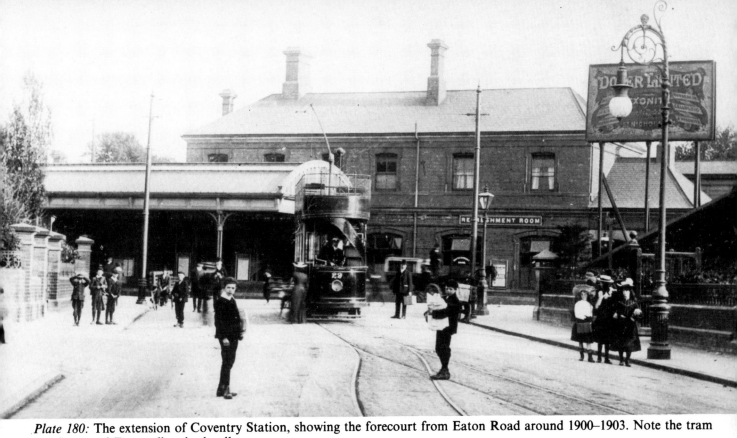

Plate 180: The extension of Coventry Station, showing the forecourt from Eaton Road around 1900–1903. Note the tram terminus, and Eton-collared schoolboys.

Coventry City Library

Plate 181: Coventry Station, Yard, Shed and Kenilworth branch from the air circa 1919. The coaches in the background are LNWR and show their corridor sides, while all drays in the goods yard appear to be horse-drawn; there is a tram waiting alongside the station forecourt.

Coventry City Library

Around Coventry

Plate 182: A derailment at Albany Road, Coventry, in 1904. The train was in the process of being marshalled, for an excursion for the Swift Motor Co. In the background are two LNWR 0-6-0s, while on the left is a Webb 0-6-0 Coal engine and on the right, what appears to be either a 'DX' or 18 in. goods 0-6-0.

Coventry City Library

Plate 183: Coventry loop line junction and signal box (later known as Humber Road), shortly prior to opening on 10th August 1914. To the right is Folley Lane, renamed Humber Road due to the proximity of the well-known motor factory.

Coventry City Library

Plate 184:   A Birmingham to Euston express leaves Coventry, and passes over the new loop line junction shortly before opening—note the ballast wagons in the background. The train is headed by an LNWR 'George the Fifth' class 4-4-0, then only a few years old.

Coventry City Library

Plate 185: Another view of the 1914 extension to Coventry's railway system. This is Gosford Green Yard, showing the Humber Avenue footbridge in 1914, probably July of that year as the signal arm carries a white cross, and ballast wagons stand on the running lines.

Coventry City Library

Leamington

Plate 186: The London & North Western Railway's viaduct over the river Leam at Leamington, during the early 1900s. The Webb 2-4-2 tank hauled train is unusual, in that the third vehicle appears to be a saloon.

M. Musson Collection

Plate 187: An 'up' evening two hour express is seen near Berkswell, behind a spanking 'George the Fifth' class 4-4-0 either from Bushbury Shed, Wolverhampton (13) or Camden (1). Nearly all the ninety or so engines of this class appeared at Birmingham (New Street) at one time or another.

W. Leslie Good, P. B. Whitehouse Collection

Plate 188: This scene near Berkswell, on the Birmingham to Coventry main line, shows a Whale 4-4-2 tank carrying express headlamps during a summer afternoon circa 1920. The train is possibly the 4.00 p.m. ex-New Street to Rugby service, with a through coach to Parkeston Quay, while the first coach appears to be of Great Eastern origin. This is followed by an LNWR corridor leading a four-coach inter-district set. Later this train (via Peterborough), was often of greater length, and 'Claughton' or superheated 'Precursor' hauled.

W. Leslie Good, P. B. Whitehouse Collection

Later Days on the LNWR Mainline

Plate 189: An early Edwardian view of Milford & Brockton Station, located on the LNWR main line between Colwich and Stafford.

Wolverhampton Public Library

Plate 190: **An unknown LNWR Whale 19in. goods 4-6-0 heads a 'down' freight train north of Lichfield, close to the Grouping.** Note the fish-tailed distant signal, painted red with a white stripe, just over the first of the three cattle wagons. These smaller-wheeled engines outlived their express counterparts, the 'Experiment' class, with the last of the class not being withdrawn until 1950, well into BR ownership. W. Leslie Good, P. B. Whitehouse Collection

Plate 191 (right): An unknown but named 'Claughton' class 4-6-0 locomotive heads south near Tamworth, with an 'up' morning express circa 1920. W. Leslie Good, P. B. Whitehouse Collection

Plate 192: **A summer evening shot of a 'down' express passing through Tamworth (Low Level) circa 1920. The engine is superheated 'Precursor' 4-4-0 No. 301** *Leviathan* **of 1904, which was superheated in June 1914.**

L&GRP, P. B. Whitehouse Collection

Plate 193: A view of unnamed LNWR 'Claughton' class 4-6-0 No. 69, running as new in 1920 complete with company coat of arms on the splasher. The train is a 'down' express photographed at Tamworth, of note are the large number of horse-boxes and vans attached at the front of the train.

L&GRP, P. B. Whitehouse Collection

Plate 194: An 'up' ex-Fleetwood express leaves Rugby circa 1920 behind an LNWR superheated 'Precursor' class 4-4-0, double-heading a then new and unnamed 'Prince of Wales' 4-6-0. In the background is the girder bridge carrying the Great Central Railway over the main line, and to the left the famous signal gantry. Also of interest are the containers on the leading vehicle, another indication that it is a boat train.

L&GRP, P. B. Whitehouse Collection

Plate 195: 'George the Fifth' class 4-4-0 No. 1481 *Typhon* takes an 'up' express from the Trent Valley line under the Great Central Railway at Rugby, just prior to Grouping.

L&GRP, P. B. Whitehouse Collection

Crewe over the Years

The original workshops for the Grand Junction Railway were built at Edge Hill, Liverpool, but by 1843 these had been moved to Crewe, in Cheshire, where the company (and later the LNWR) built one of the great Victorian railway towns. The first incumbent as Chief Engineer was Francis Trevethick.

Plates 196–198: These drawings, taken from the *Illustrated London News* of 1849, show early scenes at Crewe Works three years after the formation of the London & North Western Railway. The locomotives in the erecting shop are likely to be examples of the standard 2-2-2 (rear) or possibly 2-4-0 designs, depicting passenger and freight six-wheeled engines of Trevithick's early period.

Views one and two show the Fitting shop, while the third picture is an illustration of the Erecting shop.

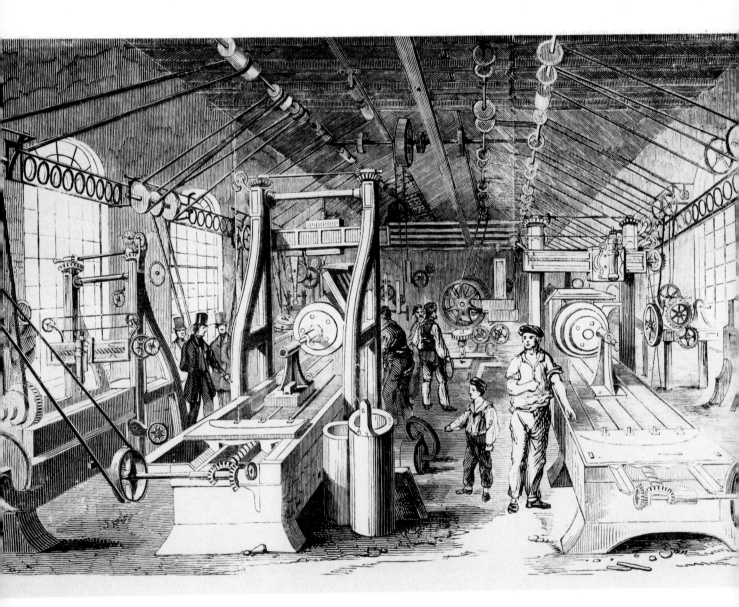

Plate 199: It goes without saying that Crewe has been an honoured name in railway history since the earliest days. In 1848, when this drawing was made, it was the northern workshop for the London & North Western Railway, as well as being a centre of communications. By this time, the Trent Valley Railway from Rugby to Stafford had been open for a year and traffic over the West Coast route then began its inexorable competition with the railways on the eastern side of England. This is the north end of the station, with the workshops visible in the background.

Crown Copyright, National Railway Museum

Plate 200: Crewe Locomotive Works, looking south towards the station in 1865. Note the standard type LNWR water/coaling stage in the background, the beginnings of the north shed to the right of the picture, the slotted signals with ringed arms for the secondary lines adjacent to the signal box, and two named locos, a 2-4-0 No. 1078 and a 2-2-2 to the right and rear of the locomotive road.

Crown Copyright, National Railway Museum

Plate 201: Rebuilt 'Newton' class 2-4-0 No. 1532 *Newton,* originally an 1866 Ramsbottom locomotive, was fitted for a while with a double chimney during draughting experiments in 1897. It is seen here in that form at Crewe.

P. B. Whitehouse Collection

Plate 202 (below): Crewe Works Yard, with two Webb engines awaiting repair, circa 1900. The 'Precedent' class 2-4-0 on the left is No. 619 *Mabel* (George Stephenson's wife), while the vacuum-fitted locomotive on the right could well be a further 'Precedent' with its splashers removed, being in for repair from Shed 14. Observe the simplicity of the cab layout. No. 619 was appropriately named to take part in the George Stephenson Centenary celebrations at Newcastle in 1881.

P. B. Whitehouse Collection

Plate 203: Crewe just prior to the Grouping, probably in 1922. This was a very typical evening sight for many years, with engines waiting to take over for the long hard pull north. In this scene, Francis Webb's 'Precedent' class 2-4-0 No. 883 *Phantom* of 1877 pilots an unknown 'Claughton' class 4-6-0.

P. B. Whitehouse Collection

Plate 204: From 1st January 1922, the London & North Western Railway amalgamated with the Lancashire & Yorkshire Railway, bringing the Hughes 4-6-0 locomotives to Crewe for trials on the main line as new management settled in. Just out of period, but still in old company colours, a Bowen-Cooke 'George the Fifth' class 4-4-0 No. 1777 *Widgeon* double-heads a L&YR 'Dreadnought' 4-6-0, southbound from Crewe on 13th October 1923.

W H. Whitworth, P. B. Whitehouse Collection

Plates 205–208: Four cab layouts of LNWR engines at Crewe Works, including Compound 2-2-2-0, a 'Precursor' 4-4-0, a 'Claughton' 4-6-0 and a Standard 0-8-0.

British Railways, P. B. Whitehouse Collection

The Rivals—Early Trams and Buses

Compared with other cities, Birmingham had a less dense railway network than usual, and its suburban services were as a consequence less well developed. In the pre-electric and motor era these services did well enough, and some continued to flourish such as the GWR Leamington-Birmingham/Stourbridge route, and the LMS New Street-Sutton-Four Oaks service. However, from about 1900, and even more so after around 1907 when the first electric tram and the early motor buses were established, the suburban rail services were in some cases hard hit, despite the lack of good tramway connections in Birmingham. In horse bus and tram days, the rail services had the edge over their competitors, but in the 1880s the steam trams took over on the main roads, with battery-electric vehicles on Bristol Road and cable cars on the Handsworth route. Also, as Birmingham's suburban stations did not lie convenient to the main roads, they became an easy prey once the steam trams had given way to the faster and cleaner electric cars.

Horse bus services, which were operated frequently as a 'second string' to some other business by private-owners, began in the 1830s while horse trams to Hockley and New Inns, and later Bournbrook, took the road in the 1870s. The steam trams arrived in 1882, the Handsworth cable cars in 1888 and the Bristol Road battery cars in 1890. Unlike horse traction, these systems could be 'switched off' when not in use, whereas the horse had to be fed and watered when not on the road and consumed all the profits, or so it was said.

Overhead electric trams in the area were first seen in Walsall, run by the South Staffordshire Tramways Co. Ltd., as far back as 1893. Birmingham's first overhead electric cars were introduced on Bristol Road in 1901, owned by the City of Birmingham Tramways Co. Ltd., while Birmingham Corporation's first electric cars took the road on the Aston route in 1904. The Birmingham Motor Express Co. put some open top motor buses on the Hagley Road service in 1903, but were absorbed by the Birmingham & Midland (later Midland Red) in 1904. Birmingham Corporation did not operate motor buses until 1913, by which time they were operating all tramway and bus routes inside the City, with private Company trams and buses running in from outside.

After World War I, some time was required to bring the run-down tramways up to standard. Birmingham was still thinking in terms of tramway extensions and the few new buses were still open top. In 1923 the first fully-enclosed Birmingham standard bogie cars (637 class) appeared. However, by the end of the decade, the bus was in the ascendant and the Black Country trams had virtually disappeared.

Plate 209: A Birmingham & District Tramways Co. Ltd. standard gauge horse tram of 1872, used for the Monmouth Street (now Colmore Row) to New Inns and Villa Cross service. These cars operated from a depot in Lozells road, still in existence in 1982, and of note is the 'knifeboard' top deck seating.

P. B. Whitehouse Collection

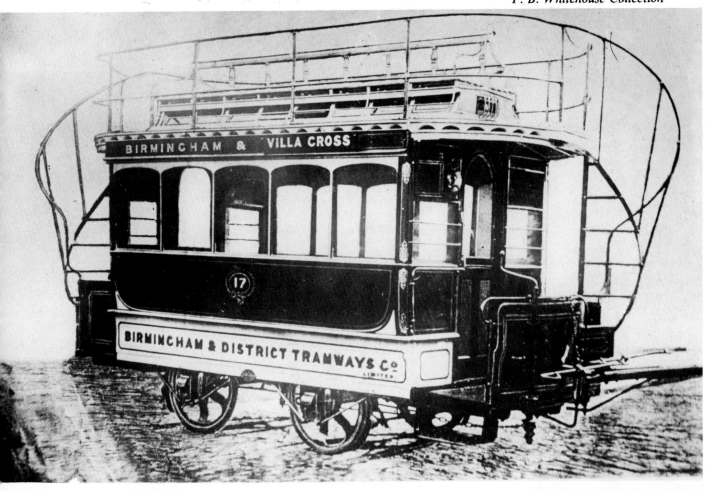

Plate 210: A City of Birmingham Tramways Co. Ltd. (CBT) two-horse bus, with 'bank engine' or trace horse attached for the pull up to Tyseley. This bus carries the 'wheel and magnet' device of the British Electric Traction Co. Ltd. (BET) on the wai: panel, the BET being the owning company of the CBT Co. Ltd. This bus has 'garden' or transverse upper deck seats.

P. B. Whitehouse Collectio

Plate 211: This Kitson steam tram locomotive and trailer, No. 18, was photographed at Moseley around 1900. The top dec roof was to protect passengers from the smuts thrown up by the engine as much as from the weather, although the sides we: unglazed. The Kings Heath steam trams operated from a depot in Silver Street, now occupied by the Midlands Electrici: Board.

P. B. Whitehouse Collectio

ate 212 (right): This City of Birm-
gham Tramways Co. Ltd. electric
r of 1901 is shown on Bristol
oad, at the corner of Priory Road,
d is mounted on a Peckham Canti-
ver truck. Some of these cars
ssed into Birmingham Corpor-
ion ownership in 1912, but not No.
3. The Bristol Road cars ran from
depot in Dawlish Road, Selly Oak.
P. B. Whitehouse Collection

ate 213 (below): An open top
WR bus, which connected Stour-
ridge with the Worcestershire vil-
ges of Hagley, Clent and Bel-
roughton, although Hagley was
ready served by a station on the
orcester to Stourbridge line.
M. Bray Collection

GREAT WESTERN RAILWAY.
STOURBRIDGE STATION & BELBROUGHTON,
VIA HAGLEY & CLENT.

Plate 214: A Clarkson steam bus of November 1904, registered at Wolverhampton and used to run the service between Bridgnorth and Wolverhampton Station. The photograph, however, appears to have been taken in the area of the square near Paddington Station.

P. B. Whitehouse Collection